Taking
the Path
of Zen

Robert Aitken

North Point Press
San Francisco
1982

The drawings of Makkōhō and Zazen positions
on pp. 17 and 18 are by Andrew Thomas.

The representation of Shakyamuni Buddha on p. 21
is courtesy of the Honolulu Academy of Arts
(Gift of Mr. Robert Allerton).

The portrait of Daitō Kokushi by Hakuin Zenji on p. 22
is reproduced courtesy of the owner, Rev.
Shūgu Yokota of Tenrin Temple, Matsue, Japan.

To the memory and to the presence of
Yasutani Hakuun-shitsu Rōdaishi

Contents

Foreword

Like a skiff slipping past heavy tankers and freighters and brightly lit tour ships, this graceful text arrives with a stiff fresh breeze behind it. Calm, clear, and useful, it presents Zen Buddhist faith and practice without mystification.

Robert Aitken is a true American Thera, Elder, "Old Teacher"—*Rōshi*—(though not so old really). Raised in Hawaii, he first came on Zen in a prison camp in Japan during World War II. As a young construction worker on Guam, he had been captured and interned as a civilian, and a guard who learned of his interest in haiku lent him R.H. Blyth's *Zen in English Literature*. Later Mr. Blyth was also placed in the camp and Aitken began the first of what would be several powerful apprenticeships. After repatriation at the end of the war, he worked in southern California and sat with Nyogen Senzaki, our most widely shared American Zen ancestor. Over forty years Robert Aitken maintained his practice, while living a life of family, universities, and jobs. After returning to Hawaii from California he made several trips to Japan, where he studied with Nakagawa Sōen Rōshi and Yasutani Hakuun Rōshi. Robert and his wife Anne became a leadership team for the growing Hawaii "Diamond Sangha." Continuing with Yasutani Rōshi's heir Yamada Kōun Rōshi, Robert and Anne made a number of further trips to Yamada Rōshi's center in Kamakura. In 1974 Robert Aitken received permission to teach, becoming a Rōshi in his own right. This book is the distillation of orientation talks developed for his students over the past ten years.

For all the fine books we've had on Zen the last two decades, not one has quite disclosed the guts and bones of how to do it, and keep doing it, as this book does. Old-timers and beginners alike will find it pulls out nails and unties knots.

Zen Buddhism is one path among many, and the first intention here is to help one choose the right path for oneself, Buddhist or other. In this spirit the fundamentals of posture, breath, and attitude are presented without theology or mythology. It often comes as a surprise to those whose image of Zen is only of spontaneity and creativity to learn of its hardworking orderliness, attention to sharpened knives and swept floors, and the demand that one be on time. Personal commitment and free strong choice become a center of this practice, rather than dependent devotion to a guru-figure or indulgence in half-grasped fancy spiritual rhetoric.

The Buddhist world is experiencing a great awakening. One of the changes comes from our modern Occidental sense of the natural validity of family life as part of the context of practice. It is exciting to see lay teachers, contemporary Vimalakirtis, who can bring the intensity of monkish training halls out to lay centers, which in turn become a source of sanity, lucidity (and good cooking!) to the daily life of neighborhoods and communities. The Zen path is for anyone, lay or priest, male or female, who is drawn to it.

Aitken Rōshi's own position, via Yamada and Yasutani Rōshi, and going back to Harada Daiun Rōshi in the early years of this century, is in the Sanbō Kyōdan lineage, the "Order of the Three Treasures." This is a recent sect of Zen that has its roots in the Sōtō school, but has incorporated much Rinzai training method as well. Aitken Rōshi is not about to suggest that we discard the traditional usages and ceremonies, the little diversities and specificities, of any lines or schools. That richness and resonance helps strengthen the devotional spirit, a needed part of any practice. Rinzai and Sōtō followers alike rejoice in the rediscovery of the elegant depths in the teachings of the great master Dōgen.

Several perplexing dualities are dealt with here. Questions of the solitary and the public, saving self and saving the world, are partially resolved by the Buddhist practice of almost always working together with others. The experiences of a solitary meditator cannot ripen without at least occasional involvement with a group of comrades who sit, cook, babysit, cut wood together in a community that accords full status and equal responsibility to women. The need for Sangha relationship is a deep implicit aspect of all Buddhism. This presents a real challenge to American self-centered individualism.

Robert Aitken has long been known for his strong feelings about militarism and war. We cannot dodge the magnitude of the problems confronting the planet, environmental, social, total. The careful walk he takes us on through the Ten Grave Precepts delivers us to the very place where changing ourselves, and the world, begins. Without blame or crippling regret, this approach liberates us to begin a work that is both individual and ultimately all-embracing.

Like an old hand-made canoe, Nordic ski, or recurve bow, this guidebook is made with great skill and care, using easily available materials, light and flexible, uniquely appropriate to the task.

Thirty years ago I was working in a logging camp in eastern Oregon and ordering an occasional book on Zen from an oriental bookstore in Pasadena. The man I dealt with was Bob Aitken and years of correspondence came of that, in Japan and back to the U.S. Those letters helped me to understand that my stubborn and cloudy bohemian radicalism needed considerable work if it were to approach anything like real compassion. I finally met Aitken Rōshi in the midseventies, resulting in a new apprenticeship for me.

Nanao Sakaki says in a poem,

> Farming in the ancient way
> Singing with coyote
> Singing against nuclear war
>   I'll never be tired of life

All of us together then: trying to follow the Way in an age of potential world holocaust is our joint spirited venture, our burden and joy. Robert Aitken Rōshi is giving us this really big rock "drenched with rain" that helps mark the way.

Gary Snyder, 1982

Preface

My purpose in this book is to provide a manual that may be used, chapter by chapter, as a program of instruction over the first few weeks of Zen training. I hope it will also serve as a reference for advanced students.

Orientation for new students of Zen is not traditional in Japan. When I attended my first Zen retreat, at Engaku Monastery in Kitakamakura, I was given no more than five minutes of instruction about how to sit and how to count my breaths before I was led into the meditation hall and shown my place. From then on it was up to me to follow the others and learn by doing. Many Zen students can relate similar experiences.

It was Harada Daiun *Rōshi,* an innovative teacher in the early part of this century, who established orientation for monks, nuns, and lay students at his monastery, and his successors have found that students who begin in this way can avoid needless trial and error in the early months, even the early years, of their practice.

Introductory talks by Yasutani Hakuun Roshi, Harada Roshi's successor, are translated in Philip Kapleau's *The Three Pillars of Zen.*[1] Yamada Kōun Roshi, Yasutani Roshi's successor, and third in leadership of this independent stream of Zen, is my own direct inspiration and personal guide.

In Harada Roshi's introductory talks, he stressed the importance of listening. If you listen as a member of an audience, you may tend to listen passively, as though I were simply expressing an opinion, not necessarily for you. This is not the act of pure listening. It is important to listen as though I were speaking to you alone.

It is the same with reading. These words are your words. They form in your mind as they appear on the page. Go with the words and you will find yourself in a natural process of acceptance and rejection that does not involve conceptual judgement.

I first prepared these talks in 1972, and they have been the core of orientation programs at our Diamond Sangha centers ever since. Down through the years, leaders and participants in these programs have offered many suggestions for revision and the book has been completely rewritten several times. I am only nominally the author now; there really should be many more names on the title page, particularly John Tarrant, and also Anne Aitken, Stephen Mitchell, P. Nelson Foster, Gary Snyder, and Yamada Roshi himself.

I am grateful to Andrew Thomas for his drawings of the *zazen* and stretching positions, to Francis Haar for photography work used in making the drawings, to Giza Juho Braun, Myphon Shoen Hunt, and Joseph B. Liggett for their typing, and to Jutta Hahne, Linda Engleberg, Michelle Hill, and Joseph B. Liggett for helping out in important ways. Thanks to Gary Snyder for his cogent foreword and to Wendell Berry for pointing out passages in the manuscript that would not be clear to someone unfamiliar with Eastern religion, and for sticking a pin in some of my inflated figures of speech.

The photograph of Śākyamuni meditating in a chair is reproduced with permission of the Honolulu Academy of Arts. This seventh-century Chinese stone figure was a gift to the Academy by Robert Allerton in 1959.

Hakuin Zenji's portrait of Daitō Kokushi is reproduced by

kindness of the owner, Rev. Shūgu Yokota of Tenrin Temple, Matsue, Japan. This painting appears in the Japanese work, *Hakuin,* edited by Naoji Takeuchi and published in Tokyo by Chikuma Shobo in 1964. Ms. Yukie Dan, secretary of the Eastern Buddhist Society in Kyoto, devoted much time to locating this painting and then arranging for its reproduction. I am very grateful to her for her successful efforts.

Finally, a note about the transcription of foreign words: I use italics and diacritical marks the first time a name or term appears and in the appendixes, but not elsewhere. Note that *ś* is pronounced "sh" in Sanskrit. Some Sanskrit words are so long that they are unreadable for anyone except specialists, so I have separated them into their components, even though this may not be exactly correct.

Taking
the Path
of Zen

This is the stone,
drenched with rain,
that marks the way.
> Santōka,
> trans. by R. H. Blyth,
> *A History of Haiku*

CHAPTER ONE

Fundamentals

> I beg to urge you, everyone:
> life-and-death is a grave matter,
> all things pass quickly away;
> each of you must be completely alert:
> never neglectful, never indulgent.[2]

This is the evening message of *sesshin* (the Zen retreat), called out by a senior member of the assembly just before lights-out. It expresses three concerns of the Zen student: first, being alive is an important responsibility; second, we have little time to fulfill that responsibility; and third, rigorous practice is necessary for fulfillment.

Our model is Shakyamuni Buddha. Known as the founder of Buddhism, he lived in India more than 2,500 years ago—but religion is fundamentally not a matter of history. I recall a course in Buddhism given by Dr. D.T. Suzuki at the University of Hawaii a long time ago. He began the course by telling the story of Shakyamuni. He did not tell it as history or biography, but as the story of Everyone—the story of you and me.

The Buddha was born a prince and it was predicted that he would become either a great religious leader or a great emperor. His father, the king, preferred to see his boy become a great emperor, so he had him trained in the arts of the warrior and the statesman. He also provided the comforts and entertain-

3

ment appropriate to the station of a young prince—fine food
and clothing, and the rest of it.

This is your story and mine. When we are young, we are all
little princes and princesses. We are each of us the center of the
universe. In fact, our mouths are the center, and everything
enters therein. We are guided by our parents toward a sense of
responsibility, but despite the program set up about us, we
emerge, each in our own way, as individual inquirers.

The Buddha's program of power and ease palled for him
before he was thirty. It is said that despite his father's efforts to
protect him from the realities of suffering, he was witness to
sickness, old age, and death. Once, he glimpsed the figure of a
monk in the palace compound and asked about him. Ponder-
ing deeply, he questioned his purpose in the world. Finally he
left his little family in care of his father to seek his spiritual
fortune in the forest.

You can imagine the difficulty of this decision. Everything
that anyone might hold dear, a beautiful spouse, a baby child,
a career as a beneficent ruler—all given up in a search that
could well lead nowhere. His decision was rooted in profound
concern for all beings. Why should there be suffering in the
world? Why should there be the weakness of old age? Why
should there be death? And what in the life of a monk might
resolve such doubts? These questions plagued the young Gau-
tama. He recognized that unless he resolved his doubts, his
leadership could not truly bring fulfillment to others.

Our childish pursuit of gratification palls and we too sense
that something we do not understand lies within all our hectic
coming and going. Our selfish ways become unsatisfying,
perhaps when we find a sexual mate. Nonetheless, I can think
of few people whose lives are completely resolved in a love
relationship, and many of us go on still further in our search for
the truth that underlies all things.

The Buddha's search led him to become a monk and to

seek instruction in philosophy and the attainment of so-called higher states of consciousness. He studied with the leading yoga teachers of his time, but remained unsatisfied. Though he could control his mind, and though he gained a complete grasp of the abstruse and subtle philosophical formulations of his time, he could not resolve the question of suffering.

In our twentieth-century Western setting, religion is not so other-worldly. It is not necessary to leave one's family to search out good teachers and it is not necessary to become a monk or nun to receive good instruction. Like the Buddha, however, we can be relentless in our pursuit of the truth we sense from the beginning. "If not here, then somewhere else, somehow else."

The Buddha went on from philosophy and mystical studies to take up asceticism. He denied himself food, sleep, shelter, and clothing. For a long period he struggled with his desires and his feelings of attachment. But this way too turned out to be a dead end. For all his self-denial he could not find true peace.

Nakagawa Sōen Roshi once said to me, "Zen is not asceticism." He said this by way of assuring me that I need not follow his example of swimming off the coast of Japan in February. But Zen is not indulgence either. The practice involves rigor and is not possible in a casual life-style. We need to find the Middle Way. The Buddha learned, and we learn also, that lengthy fasting and other kinds of excessive self-deprivation only weaken the body and spirit and make the practice more difficult. And, as the *Ts'ai Kên T'an* tells us, "Water which is too pure has no fish."[3]

So the Buddha turned back to meditation, which he had undoubtedly learned from his teachers. He took his seat beneath a Bodhi tree, determined not to rise until he had resolved all his doubts. Early one morning he happened to look up and saw the morning star. He cried out, "Oh, wonderful!

wonderful! Now I see that all beings of the universe are the *Tathāgata!* It is only their delusions and attachments which keep them from acknowledging that fact."[4]

Tathagata is another name for Buddha. It means literally, "thus come," or more fully "one who thus comes," and implies pure appearance, the absolute coming forth as the living fact. All beings are Buddha. All beings are the truth, just as they are. A great T'ang period teacher used the expression, "Just this!" to present the heart of deepest experience.[5]

This deepest experience is not available to the casual on-looker. Delusions and attachments consisting of self-centered and conceptual thinking obscure the living fact. The Zen path is devoted to clearing away these obstructions and seeing into true nature.

This can be your path, the Middle Way of *zazen,* or seated meditation. The Middle Way is not halfway between extremes, but a completely new path. It does not deny thought and it does not deny the importance of self-control, but reason and restraint are not its main points.

Dr. Suzuki used to say that Zen is noetic, by which I understand him to mean that it originates in the mind. It is not intellectual, but involves realization, the purest gnosis of "just this!" It also involves application of such realization in the daily life of family, job, and community service.

Making It Personal

In taking up Zen Buddhism, we find that the life of the Buddha is our own life. Not only Shakyamuni's life, but the lives of all the succeeding teachers in our lineage are our own lives. As Wu-mên Hui-k'ai has said, in true Zen practice our very eyebrows are tangled with those of our ancestral teachers, and we see with their eyes and hear with their ears.[6] This is not because we copy them, or change to be like them. I might explain Wu-men's words by saying that in finding our own true nature, we find the true nature of all things, which the old teachers so clearly showed in their words and actions. But the authentic experience of identity is intimate beyond explanation. And it is not only with old teachers that we find complete intimacy. The Chinese thrush sings in my heart and gray clouds gather in the empty sky of my mind. All things are my teacher.

On the Zen path, we seek for ourselves the experience of Shakyamuni. However, we do not owe fundamental allegiance to him, but to ourselves and to our environment. If it could be shown that Shakyamuni never lived, the myth of his life would be our guide. In fact it is better to acknowledge at the outset that myths and religious archetypes guide us, just as they do every religious person. The myth of the Buddha is my own myth.

Thus, it is essential at the beginning of practice to acknowledge that the path is personal and intimate. It is no good to examine it from a distance as if it were someone else's. You must walk it for yourself. In this spirit, you invest yourself in your practice, confident of your heritage, and train earnestly side by side with your sisters and brothers. It is this engagement that brings peace and realization.

Concentration

The first step on this way of personal engagement is concentration. Usually, we think of concentration as focusing on something with intense mental energy. This is not incorrect, but for the Zen student it is not complete. Even in ordinary experience, we transcend concentration. For example, what happens when you take a civil service test? If you are fully prepared, you sit down and write. Though your neighbor becomes restless, or it begins to rain outside, your attention doesn't swerve. Before you know it, you are finished. A relatively long time has passed. Suddenly you find that your back is stiff and your feet are asleep. You feel tired and you want to go home and rest. But during the course of the test, your stiffness and your tiredness did not distract you. You were absorbed in what you were doing. You became someone taking a test. You forgot yourself in your task.

Rebuilding an engine, nursing a child, watching a movie—all these acts may transcend concentration. Focusing on something involves two things, you and the object, but your everyday experience shows you that when you are truly absorbed the two melt away, and there is "not even one," as Yamada Roshi likes to say.

Accepting the Self

The everyday experiences of forgetting the self in the act of, say, fixing a faucet, may be understood as a model for zazen, the meditation practice of the Zen student. But before any forgetting is possible, there must be a measure of confidence. The diver on the high board lets everything go with each dive, but could not do so without the development of confidence, a development that goes hand in hand with training. Such letting go is not random. The diver has become one with the practice of diving—free, yet at the same time highly disciplined.

Even champion divers, however, do not touch their deepest potential simply by working out on the high board. A more useful model may be found among the archetypes of zazen, such as Mañjuśrī who occupies the central place on the altar of the *zendō* (meditation hall). He holds a scroll, representing wisdom, and a sword to cut off all your concepts. He is seated upon a recumbent lion, and both Manjushri and the lion look very comfortable. The lion power is still there, however, and when Manjushri speaks, it is with the voice of that lion. Completely free, and completely controlled! The new student must make friends with the lion and tame it before he or she can take the lion seat. This takes time and patience.

At first this inner creature seems more like a monkey than a lion, greedily snatching at bright-colored objects and jumping around from one thing to another. Many people blame themselves, even dislike themselves, for their restless behavior. But if you reject yourself, you are rejecting the agent of realization. So you must make friends with yourself. Enjoy yourself. Take comfort in yourself. Smile at yourself. You are developing confidence.

Don't misunderstand. I am not directing you to the way of pride and selfishness. I point to the way of Bashō, who loved himself and his friends with no pride at all:

> At our moonviewing party
> there is no one
> with a beautiful face.

I commented on quoting this poem elsewhere: "What homely bastards we are, sitting here in the moonlight!"[7] This kind of humorous, deprecatory self-enjoyment is the true basis for responsibility, the ability to respond. When you make a mistake, do you punish yourself or can you shake your head with a smile and learn something in the process? If you curse yourself, you are postponing your practice. If you simply tick off the error and resolve to do better the next time, then you are ready to practice.

If Shakyamuni Buddha had dwelled upon his own inadequacies rather than the question of suffering in the world, he would never have realized that everything is all right from the beginning. Zazen is not the practice of self-improvement, like a course in making friends and influencing people. With earnest zazen, character change does occur, but this is not a matter of ego-adjustment. It is forgetting the self.

Yamada Roshi has said, "The practice of Zen is forgetting the self in the act of uniting with something." This does not mean that you should try to get rid of your self. That is not possible except by suicide, and suicide is the greatest pity, for you, like each other being of the universe, are unique, the Tathagata coming forth in your particular form as essential nature.

Forgetting the self is the presentation of uniqueness. See how particularly himself the mime Marcel Marceau becomes when he forgets himself in his work. And that is *his* work—we each of us are particularly ourselves when we forget ourselves as we change a tire, or whatever. Forgetting the self is the act of just doing the task, with no self-consciousness sticking to the action.

Breath Counting

Zazen is a matter of just doing it. However, even for the advanced Zen student, work on the meditation cushions is always being refined. It is like learning to drive a car. At first everything is mechanical and awkward. You consciously depress the clutch and shift into low, then release the clutch gradually while depressing the gas pedal, steering to stay within the white lines and to avoid other cars. There are so many things to remember and to do all at once, that at first you make mistakes and perhaps even have an accident. But when you become one with the car, you are more confident. And you become a better and better driver with experience.

The preliminary method on the way of Zen is the process of counting the breaths, as it is for many other illuminative schools of Asian religion. Once, at our Koko An Zendo in Honolulu, we were hosts to a *Theravāda* Buddhist teacher from Sri Lanka. We asked him how he taught meditation to his disciples, and he proceeded to demonstrate to us the same techniques of counting the breaths which we had learned from our own Japanese Zen teacher. It is somehow the natural first step. The breath is both a spontaneous part of our physical system and, to some degree, under our control. In early days of our Western culture, breath was considered our very spirit, as our words, "inspiration" and "expiration" show clearly. When we "expire," once and for all, we have ended our inspiration for this life.

In the next chapter, I will give a detailed exposition of Zen method. For now, it is sufficient simply to try to count your breaths. Sit with your back straight, and count "one" for the inhalation, "two" for the exhalation, "three" for the next inhalation, "four" for the next exhalation, and so on up to "ten," and repeat. Don't go above "ten" because it is too difficult to keep track of higher numbers. You are not exercising your thinking faculty in this practice; you are developing your power to invest in something.

Counting is the first mental exercise you learned as a child. It is the easiest of all formal, mental efforts, the closest to being second nature. I have seen people who have migrated to a new country and adjusted themselves fully to their adopted culture and language, still counting their bills at the bank with the numbers of their childhood: *un deux trois quatre; ichi ni san shi.*

But though breath counting is natural, you cannot dream at it and just let it happen. Truly to meet the challenge of your rampaging mind, you must devote all your attention just to "one," just to "two." When (not if!) you lose the count and you finally realize that you have lost it, come back to "one" and start over.

Many people can count to "ten" successfully the first few times they try, but no one who has not practiced can maintain the sequence for long. Though one needs a disciplined mind even for quite ordinary purposes, such as conducting business or teaching, few of us have the faculty of extended attention. I have had people tell me after trying zazen for twenty-five minutes, "You know, I never even got to 'one'!" Counting the breaths shows us that indeed, as a Chinese proverb says, the mind is like a wild horse.

Breath counting is not the kindergarten of Zen. For many

students it is a full and complete lifetime practice. But even with just a month of practice, a few minutes each day, you will be able to focus more clearly on your work or study and to give yourself more freely to conversation and recreation. You will have learned how to begin, at any rate, the task of keeping yourself undivided, for it is thinking of something other than the matter at hand that separates us from reality and dissipates our energies.

CHAPTER TWO

Method

Zen Buddhism is one path among many. I have heard it said that all paths lead to the top of the same mountain. I doubt it. I think that one mountain may seem just a small hill from the top of another. Let one hundred mountains rise! Meanwhile you must find your own path, and your own mountain. You may have an experience of some kind that points the direction clearly, or you may have to explore for a while. But eventually you will have to settle on a particular way, with a particular teacher.

Trusting yourself to a specific path naturally involves risks. Unquestioning acceptance might lead you to blind belief in something quite unhealthy. You should be sure that a given path is worthy of your investment. The process of deciding, "This is (*or* is not) the way for me," takes time. At any Zen center worthy of the name, no one will rush you. In a true *dōjō* (training center), evidence of worth will be found at every hand, and you will soon reach the point of trust.

Zazen as Experiment

The heart of Zen training is zazen. Without zazen, there is no Zen, no realization, and no application of the practice. It has its roots in earliest Vedic times and was probably well-established by Shakyamuni's day. It has since been refined by trial and error in countless training centers through some

13

ninety generations of Zen teachers. By now its form is well established.

Yet the mind remains vast and creative. Words of our ancestors in the Dharma (teaching) turn out to be helpful, but the way itself is still guided by experiment.

We are concerned with realizing the nature of being, and zazen has proved empirically to be the practical way to settle down to the place where such realization is possible. This is not a way that is designed for Japanese, for intelligentsia, or for any particular class or category of individuals. The fact that zazen originates in India and China, and that it comes to us through Korea and Japan is not so very important. As North Americans, Australians, Europeans, we make it our own.

There is a further important point. Zazen is not merely a means, any more than eating, sleeping, or hugging your children are means or method. Dōgen Kigen Zenji said, "Zazen is itself enlightenment."[8] This unity of ends and means, effect and cause, is the *tao* (way) of the Buddha, the practice of realization.

The Posture

I have heard that someone asked Sasaki Jōshū Roshi, "What of Zen is necessary to preserve?" He replied, "Posture and the breathing." I think I might say simply, "Posture."

Posture is the form of zazen. To avoid fatigue and to permit consciousness to settle, legs, seat, and spine should support the body. If strain is thrown on the muscles and tendons of the back and neck, it will be impossible to continue the practice beyond a short period.

We may take our model from the posture of a one-year-old baby. The child sits bolt upright, with spine curving forward slightly at the waist, rather than completely straight up-and-down. The belly sticks out in front, while the rear end sticks out behind. Sitting with the spine completely straight at this age would be impossible, as the muscles are still undeveloped—too weak to hold the body erect. Curved forward, the vertebrae are locked into their strongest position, and the child can forget about staying erect.

When you take your seat on your cushions, or on a chair if your legs don't bend easily, your spine should curve forward slightly at the waist like the baby's. Your belt should be loose, and your stomach be allowed to hang out naturally, while your posterior is thrust back for solid support. Katsuki Sekida, former resident advisor to the Diamond Sangha, once sent out New Year cards with the greeting, "Belly forward, buttocks back." This is how we should greet the New Year, or the new day.

If the spine is correctly positioned, then all else follows naturally. Head is up, perhaps bent forward very slightly. Chin is in, ears are on line with the shoulders, and shoulders are on line with the hips.

The Legs

Legs are a problem. Few people, even children, even in Japan, are flexible enough to sit easily in a lotus position without painful practice. Our tendons and muscles need stretching over many months before we can be comfortable. Yet, in the long run, sitting with one or both feet in the lap is far superior to sitting in any other position. In that way you are locked into your practice and your organs are completely at ease. Sitting in a chair, however, may be the only option for one suffering from injury or arthritis.

Certain exercises are helpful in stretching for the lotus positions. Begin by sitting on a rug or pad:

1. Bring heels of both feet to the crotch, and bend forward with your back straight and touch your face to the floor, placing your hands on the floor just above your head. Knees also should touch the floor in this exercise and if they do not, rock them gently up and down, stretching the ligaments.

2. Bring your feet together with your legs outstretched,

bend forward and touch your hands to the floor by your feet, keeping your back and legs straight; if possible, touch your face to your knees.

3. Extend your legs as far apart as possible. Bend forward with your back and legs straight and touch your face to the floor, placing your hands on the floor, either outstretched or just above your head.

4. Double back one leg so that your foot is beside your seat, with your instep, shin, and knee resting on the rug or pad. Bend the other leg back in the same way. Now lie back on one elbow, then on both elbows, and finally lie back flat. At first you may have to lie back against a sofa cushion so that you are not completely flat, and perhaps have someone to help you. If you can manage to lie flat, raise your arms over your head until your hands touch the floor and then bring them to your side again.

Yasutani Roshi did these exercises every morning before breakfast, well into his eighties. It may take you some time to become flexible enough to do them even partially. Maintain the effort and your zazen will be less demanding physically.

These four exercises are the core of *Makkōhō,* a Japanese system of physical conditioning. Don't push yourself too hard or you may strain a muscle or pull a ligament. At the limit of each stretch, breathe in and out three or four times and try to relax.[9]

Cushions

Correct zazen posture requires the use of a cushion and a pad. The pad is at least 28 inches square, stuffed with kapok or cotton batting so that it is about 1½ inches thick. The *zafu,* or cushion, completes the setup. It is spherical, stuffed with kapok; 12 inches or more in diameter, and it flattens out somewhat in use. Ordinary pillows may be substituted for it, but they are not as practical. Foam rubber is sometimes used to fill

Makkōhō Position 1

Makkōhō Position 2

Makkōhō Position 3

Makkōhō Position 4

Full Lotus

Half Lotus

Seiza

Burmese

the pad, but it makes an unsteady seat. It cannot be used for the zafu.

The zafu elevates your rear end. This makes for correct posture without straining. I have known yogis who could take the full lotus position standing on their heads, but few who could meditate for twenty-five minutes without a cushion.

Getting Seated

Bring the zafu to the back edge of the pad, sit on it, and rest both knees on the pad. For the lotus position, place your right foot on your left thigh, as high as possible, and then your left foot on your right thigh. The half lotus is simply the left foot on the right thigh, while the right foot is drawn up under the left thigh. The full lotus is the most secure way to sit. The half lotus is adequate; it will distort the body slightly, but not enough to matter. It is all right to place the right foot on the left thigh by way of compensating for a spinal deviation or as relief during sesshin.

There are two other possibilities. One is the Burmese style, in which one leg is placed in front of the other, so that both ankles are resting on the pad. This position is not quite as steady as half lotus, but it is easier on the knees. As you get used to it, you may be able to start taking up half lotus for brief intervals at first, and then for longer periods.

The other option is the *seiza* position, which is something like kneeling, except that your rear end is supported by a zafu. Some people turn the zafu on edge before sitting on it. This keeps the legs closer together and is more comfortable. Your weight rests on your seat, knees, shins, and ankles. Like the Burmese position, seiza is not as secure as half lotus, but it may be used as a kind of intermediate practice while the legs are becoming more flexible through daily stretching exercises. It is also useful as a relief during sesshin.

The one most desperately uncomfortable position is the

conventional cross-legged, or tailor-fashion of sitting. Both feet are under the thighs. The back is rounded; the belly is drawn in. The shin of one leg rests on the ankle of the other, and severe pain is inevitable. The lungs must labor to draw in their air and other organs seem cramped as well. Sitting in this way is probably not conducive to good health or to good practice.

The incomplete half lotus, in which the upper foot rests on the calf of the other leg, rather than upon the thigh, also may be painful after a while, not in the legs, but in the back. Somehow, it is difficult to be fully erect in this position, and one must strain in the effort.

All these suggestions about leg positions should be taken as guidelines, not as rules. Do the best you can, and no more will be asked. One of our members at the Maui Zendo did a full seven-day sesshin flat on her back. She had ruptured a disk, and could not even sit up without assistance. Daitō Kokushi, great master of early Japanese Zen, had a withered leg and could not sit in any of the conventional ways.

Hakuin Zenji's idealized portrait of Daito Kokushi shows him seated with a suspicious bump under his robe where his feet would be. I am not sure whether or not this represents his lame leg. In any case, it is said that he was only able to bring that leg to its correct place on his thigh at the end of his life.

"All my life I have been obeying you," he said to his leg. "Now you obey me!" With a mighty heave, he brought his leg into position, breaking it, and dying in the same moment.

I recommend against such drastic practice, at least until you are ready to die. The full lotus position is the most secure way to sit, but it is also the one most likely to injure the overeager beginner. Your legs should be fairly flexible before you attempt it, and even then, don't sit in that way for long periods until you are fairly comfortable. You may "pop your knee," and this may result in permanent damage.

Shakyamuni Buddha seated in a chair.

Daitō Kokushi, a portrait by
Hakuin Ekaku Zenji.

A yoga teacher advised me that people should be careful to support their knees with their hands when placing their legs in position for zazen, and when unfolding them at the end of a period. This is cogent advice. The knees are comparatively weak joints.

Eyes and Hands

Your eyes should be about two-thirds closed, cast down, looking at a point about three feet ahead of you. It should be remembered that if your eyes are closed, you may become dreamy; if your eyes are wide open, you will be too easily distracted. Also, don't try to keep your eyes focused. After a while you will find that they naturally go out of focus whenever you sit.

Place your hands in your lap in the meditation *mudrā*. Your left hand should rest, palm upward, on the palm of your right hand, and your thumbs should touch, forming an oval. (It is said, technically, that it is the tips of your thumbnails that should touch.) Your hands should rest in your lap, just touching your belly, and your elbows should project a little. Some Zen teachers suggest that you imagine you are holding a precious jewel in your hands; others suggest that you place your attention there. In any case, the hand position is critically important, for it reflects the condition of your mind. If your mind is taut, your thumbs will hold the oval; if your mind becomes dull or strays into fantasy, your thumbs will tend to collapse. (Note that in the Rinzai School, the hands are merely clasped together, with the right hand holding the left thumb.)

Beginning Your Practice

When you sit down, place your feet in position, lean far forward, thrust your posterior back, and sit up. Next, take a deep silent breath and hold it. Then exhale slowly and silently, all the way out, and hold it. Breathe in deeply again and hold it, and all the way out once more. You may do this through the mouth, but note that at all other times you should breath through the nose. These two deep inhalations and exhalations help to cut the continuity of your mental activity and to quiet the mind for zazen.

Now rock from side to side, widely at first, then in decreasing arcs. Lean forward and back in the same way, and you will find that you are well settled and ready to begin your breath counting. Follow the instructions I gave you earlier. Count "one" for the inhalation, "two" for the exhalation, and so on up to "ten," and repeat.

More on Breath Counting

You will find breath counting to be a useful means throughout your life of Zen training. Whatever your practice becomes later on, you should count your breaths from "one" to "ten," one or two sequences, at the start of each new period of zazen. It will help you to settle down, and will serve to remind you that you are not just sitting there, but sitting with a particular practice.

At best, you become one with your object in zazen, so if you merely sit with a focus, you tend to close off your potential. You and your object remain two things. Become each point, each number, in the sequence of counting. You and the count and the breath are all of a piece in *this* moment. Invest yourself in each number. There is only "one" in the whole universe, only "two" in the whole universe, just that single point. Everything else is dark.

At first, as a beginner, you will be conscious of each step in the procedure, but eventually you will become the procedure itself. The practice will do the practice. It takes time, and for months, perhaps, you will seem to spend your time dreaming rather than counting. This is normal. Your brain secretes thoughts as your stomach secretes pepsin. Don't condemn yourself for this normal condition.

Breath counting is only one of many devices you can use in your practice. Later I will discuss some others with you in detail.

CHAPTER THREE

Appropriate Means

Teaching in Zen Buddhism is a presentation. It is not merely a device intended to bring about a certain pedagogical result. Teaching is the Tathagata. Examples of this would be the Buddha twirling a flower before his assembly, with no words and no explanations, or Chü-chih holding up one finger whenever he was asked a question.[10]

There is a lot of misunderstanding about this, even among Zen students themselves. Many suppose, for example, that *kōans,* or Zen themes, are riddles designed to throw you into a dilemma, and that this sets up a psychological process that leads to a kind of breakthrough called realization. While it is true that you may feel frustration in koan work, and you do experience a release with realization, fundamentally the koan is a particular expression of Buddha nature and your koan work is simply a matter of making that expression clear to yourself and to your teacher.

In Sanskrit, elements of teaching are called *upāya,* or "appropriate means." In Sino-Japanese, this term is rendered *hō-ben,* and both words refer to the various presentations of Buddha nature that we can take up as guides on our journey. Not only do we find inspiration from the upaya of others but we ourselves come forth compassionately with appropriate means as we interact with family and colleagues.

Still More on Breath Counting

Breath counting is one such upaya, and by now you have learned what a great challenge it is. You find how much energy you habitually channel to your thinking faculties and how readily you can drift off into planning, remembering, or fantasizing. Still, most people live out their lives in their work, in their families, and in their fantasy. They have no energy left for deeper questions about their own being, and they may even use relatively superficial activities to obscure such questions.

Thus you may find yourself an adult unable even to attend well enough to count from "one" to "ten." Or perhaps with great care you can do it once, but then you lose track in the next sequence. Or you may find that you do the count mechanically on one level while dreaming on another. Now you can see the importance of training. If your monkey-mind will not let you examine each step in a simple sequence of breaths, then how can you sustain the attention necessary to see into your own nature?

You may find that you consistently lose the count at "four" or "six" or "eight." Try setting your first target at that number, whatever it is. Perhaps you may have to begin with just "two." Count "one, two;" "one, two," until you have mastered that much concentration. Then gradually extend your goal to higher numbers until you can attain the full count of ten, more or less consistently.

All of us fear failure, to one degree or another, and prefer not to try something that seems too difficult. This device of adjusting your goal to your present capacity is one by which you can avoid unnecessary frustration at the outset of your practice. However, it is important to understand that Zen training is also a matter of coping with failure. Everybody fails at first, just as Shakyamuni Buddha did. Zazen, for anyone who is not completely mature, is a matter of checking delusion and returning to the practice, checking and returning, over and over.

When your mind shifts to some unfinished business, return to your counting. If it is important, you will remember it again when your zazen is ended. If you feel happy about something, that is all right, continue your breath counting in that happy condition. But when you dwell upon the happiness itself, then you lose the count. Likewise, you may feel sad. That is all right too. Just continue counting with that sad feeling. But if you seek out the cause of your sadness, the count disappears. Zazen has a therapeutic effect, but it is not itself therapy.

Above all, don't say to yourself, "Oh, what's the matter with me! There I go again, dreaming when I should be counting!" Such recrimination is itself a delusion. Simply and quietly drop your train of thought when you notice that you are straying and come back to your count.

The Zen Center Organization

The organization of friends who do zazen together is an appropriate means for the practice. If we deny teacher, fellow students, and our spiritual home, we are stuck in an empty place. Though the world is our home in a larger sense, we need a supportive local environment in which we can engage ourselves. Without support on the one hand and engagement on the other, personal fulfillment is not really possible. The Zen Buddhist organization is entirely directed toward enabling the student to see into his or her true nature, and to apply that insight in daily life. The way the dojo is arranged, its schedule and rules, and the style of behavior of the members—all are intended as the tao of the Buddha.

Outside every Rinzai Zen monastery in Japan is a sign that announces the name of the temple, the name of the mountain (even in the city, the temple has a "mountain" or place name), the name of its headquarter temple, and the name of its subsect. All this is followed by the words *Semmon Dōjō,* which means "Special Training Center." Once you have located your special training center, you can agree with your antisectarian friends that everywhere can be a temple. But until then, everywhere is also nowhere.

The *Hua Yen Sūtra* describes the universe as the "Net of Indra," a multidimensional net in which every knot is a jewel that shines forth alone, and yet fully reflects each other jewel.[11] The Sangha, or fellowship, is the Net of Indra in miniature. We polish our own jewel in zazen and reflect those of students about us.

Ritual

The rituals and ceremonies of Zen practice may be understood in a number of ways. For present purposes, let me offer only two primary explanations. First, ritual helps us to deepen our religious spirit and to extend its vigor to our lives. Second, ritual is an opening for the experience of forgetting the self as the words or the action become one with you, and there is nothing else.

Gasshō would be the simplest illustration of the first point. This is the act of placing your hands palm to palm, so that the tips of your forefingers are an inch from your nose. We bow with our hands at gassho as we enter or leave the dojo, and before zazen we bow in this way twice at our seats, once to our sisters and brothers beside us, and once to sisters and brothers on the opposite side of the dojo.

Gassho is a sign of joining together in respect. In South Asia and Southeast Asia, gassho is the conventional greeting between friends. In our practice, it is the sign that we join respectfully with our sisters and brothers, with the great figures of our lineage, and with our training itself.

Also, sometimes we bow to the floor and raise our hands a few inches. We are lifting the Buddha's feet over our heads. It is a sign of throwing everything away, or as one of my students described it, the act of pouring everything out from the top of the head. All our self-concern, all our preoccupations are thrown away completely. There is just that bow.

"Just that bow" presents the second point. You have been practicing on your cushions to become one with something. Then at a particular moment you forget yourself in conjunction with some incident. It may be something you do, or something you notice outside yourself. That sound, that act of standing up, or whatever, is then all that is. The entire universe is otherwise silent and empty.

Dogen Zenji expressed this experience of forgetting as "Body and mind fall away; the fallen away body and mind."[12] It is a single event, but for purposes of explication we can identify two aspects and give them traditional names. When you fall away, that is "Great Death," and with this abrupt sloughing off, you are the person who has fallen away. You find the "Great Life," as you sit down, laugh at a joke, or drink a glass of water—free of body and mind, yet functioning as body and mind.

Thus in the ritual of the dojo, in the same atmosphere of devotion that is the environment of zazen, the signals of bells and clappers, the order of eating a meal, the sutras and the bows, all encourage the experience of falling away. Without any preoccupation with meaning, you may, as have some students that I know, find the sutras reciting themselves. Just reciting, the self is truly forgotten, and your perspective on the world is turned around 180 degrees.

Schedule

A welter of things present themselves to us for our attention. Unless we are personally organized, we are at the mercy of circumstances and incidents that push us about day by day throughout our lives. The source of personal disorganization lies in our habits of thinking, and we seek to quiet our busy minds in zazen. But unless we correct disorganization in our daily routine as well, our practice will be hit or miss, often poorly focused.

The schedule at a training center or in the life of the Zen student living at home is the posture of time, the spine of time. Just as you are free to apply yourself fully to breath counting when your sitting posture is correct, breath after breath, so you can freely and easily move from work to play to zazen to sleep and so on, investing yourself in each, when your schedule is balanced and stable.

At home, you will have to fix a schedule for yourself. The best arrangement is one designed to minimize decision making. It may seem a denial of human dignity and maturity to minimize the number of decisions you have to make, but the fact is that streamlining your life in this way will allow you to turn your full energies to your practice. Just cooking, just typing, just resting, just sitting—taking each thing in its turn with full attention is your practice, on the cushions or off.

Yün-mên Wên-yen said, "The world is so vast and wide. Why do you put on your priest's robe at the sound of the bell?"[13] The bell signals a lecture in the main hall of the monastery. The monks put on their formal robes and make their way from their quarters to hear their teacher speak. Yun-men's question is a koan and requires a fundamental response, but as an upaya I may ask, "Why don't you pick up your towel and go to the beach when you hear the sound of the bell?" The world is very wide. There are many options. When the alarm clock rings, why do you get up? Is it just because you know you will be fired if you are late to work?

Zazen may be considered a matter of signals too. Each breath is full and complete in itself, but while we are learning to concentrate each breath can be a signal to maintain the practice. The first signal is "one," the second signal is "two." If you disregard the signals and say to yourself, "No, at this breath I won't count; I'll think about my social problems," then you are separating yourself from the practice, saying, in effect, "I am too good for zazen."

In the same way, we train ourselves to find our true nature by ignoring the egocentric whims that say, "No, I will sleep in this morning," or "No, I don't feel like zazen just now." Unless we invest in our practice of breath counting, typing, washing dishes, or whatever, and in our movement from activity to activity, we find ourselves cut off from ourselves, a very miserable condition.

Sitting with Others

It is important to sit with others, but many people sit alone because they have no choice. In such circumstances you can gain strength and independence in your practice, but you will find encouragement and support by corresponding with other Zen students, and by subscribing to newsletters of the various Zen centers. Choose the center that you like best from your contacts by mail and try to get away for sesshin there at least once a year.

Inquire at the department of religion at your nearest university about Zen groups in your area. You may find that people are doing zazen together nearby. If not, consider starting your own sitting group. If even one friend is interested, the two of you can become a true Sangha. The Diamond Sangha began when Anne Aitken and I started sitting with two friends once a week in our living room. We used sofa cushions as zafu and for a bell we struck a Pyrex bowl with a wooden spoon.

With realization you find that the other is none other than yourself. By joining a Sangha you acknowledge this from the beginning. So even if you feel that you prefer to sit alone, experiment with sitting in a group. You may find that your reflection in others is an encouragement to your practice.

When you do sit alone, heed Shaku Sōen Zenji's advice to remember that you are sitting together with all beings in the universe.[14] Put this thought foremost in your consciousness just as you take your seat.

When to Sit

Set a time each day when you won't be disturbed. For many, early morning is best. The house is quiet, and traffic sounds are at a minimum. Evening is also a possible time, but guests may appear or your family may have other plans.

Actually, any time, except just after a meal, is a good time. Eager students sometimes even sit after meals, ignoring the slight discomfort of a full stomach. Mothers or fathers of young children may find that naptime is their only chance, often a haphazard chance. But if possible, set the same time each day. This may be circumstance time, not necessarily clock time. If your circumstance time is after you get up and wash, then place yourself on your cushions every day at that time. Never allow yourself to miss.

How Long to Sit

Don't try to sit too long at first. Five minutes may be enough to start with. If you sit religiously every day for five minutes, you will soon wish to extend your time to longer periods. But if you try to start off with half an hour, you may give up after the first day. You will be like the person who becomes concerned about physical condition and decides to jog two miles—but that is likely to be the end of it. This is the error of the perfectionist. Bring your targets up close so that you can hit the bull's-eye each time and then, gradually, move them to greater distances for greater achievements.

Though periods of sitting vary in length from center to center, it was Yasutani Roshi's opinion that you should not try to sit more than twenty-five minutes without a break, even as a veteran of zazen. I agree. If you wish to sit for a long time, break after twenty-five minutes, rise and stretch, wash your face, or just look at the sky, and then return to your seat. You will find yourself refreshed. Sitting for long periods without moving can cause you to become stale, sometimes without knowing it.

It may be helpful to use a kitchen timer, so that you need not check your watch as you meditate. Cover it with something so that its ticking will not be a disturbance. The traditional way is to sit for the time it takes a stick of incense to burn. The shorter sticks sold commercially burn for just about twenty-five minutes.

The Place and Its Spirit

Your place, too, should be fixed. Most of us cannot afford a separate room for zazen, but all of us can make a corner sacred. Put your pad and cushion there, with a low table or shelf for incense, flowers, and a picture of Shakyamuni, Bodhidharma, Kanzeon, or one of the other great Bodhisattvas or teachers in our lineage. The room should be clean and tidy, without too much sunlight, though of course it should not be gloomy either. The spirit of religious dedication that is so apparent in the atmosphere of a training center can thus be evoked in your own home and in your daily life.

On the one hand, this religious setting should be spare— free from sentimental feeling that leads to self-preoccupation.

The incense, for example, should not be sticky-sweet. On the other hand, your setting for zazen should not be so arid that it has no religious associations. Some people find incense and pictures of the Buddha to be a threat to their rational spirit. But we most certainly cannot depend solely upon our rationality.

Incense, pictures, and flowers help to put us in touch with the wellsprings of universal spirit, drawing us to the oneness with our heritage and with our sisters and brothers which we already know intellectually to be the fact of our practice. They help us to establish meaningful archetypes of compassion and realization in our innermost being. Without such aids, zazen may become just a kind of pop psychology exercise, on a level with books devoted to positive thinking.

Dress

Dress in clean clothes when you sit. Yasutani Roshi advises against sitting in pajamas, for the association with sleep or casual manner may carry over into zazen. Keep your shoulders covered, and choose colors that will not be distracting. At most training centers, students will be asked not to wear patterned clothing, and to avoid perfume and noticeable jewelry.

To insure circulation of blood in your legs, it is better not to wear tight-fitting trousers or socks. A zazen robe or gown, or the Japanese dress of kimono and *hakama,* is best.

Kinhin

In the training center, we do *kinhin* between periods of zazen. This is the practice of walking formally at a slow, moderate or even rapid pace, depending on the custom of the center, while continuing to count the breaths or to work on a koan. At centers in Harada Roshi's lineage, we walk with the right hand clenched lightly about the thumb, placed near the solar plexus, with the left hand covering it. Elbows project a little, and forearms are parallel to the floor. These details vary in other traditions.

When the bell rings at the end of the period of zazen, rock back and forth a few times in increasing arcs, then swing around on your cushion in the direction of the altar and stand up slowly with your back to your pad, placing your feet firmly on the floor. Do not stand on your pad. It is soft and if your feet are asleep you may turn your ankle. When a bell sounds, bow with your hands at gassho, return your hands to your chest, turn left, and after a moment's pause step out.

Kinhin is, we may say, halfway between the quality of attention demanded by sitting and the quality of attention demanded in the everyday world. You are doing zazen while walking, but you must also be careful to keep up with the person ahead of you. The term "kinhin" means "sutra-walking," the sutra that is walked rather than read aloud. In ancient days, sutras were actually recited while walking and in special ceremonies they still are. Kinhin shows us that our everyday actions are themselves sutras.

You will be able to practice kinhin in everyday life to some extent. Walking from your home to the bus, from your house to the garden, and within the house, you can touch your hands together and place yourself in the dimension of zazen. Priests, nuns, and serious lay people of many world religions practice a kind of formal or informal kinhin. It is known in these traditions that touching the hands together while walking helps place you in a mood of devotion.

But don't allow your practice to draw inquisitive attention. There is no need to make a display of zazen, kinhin, and other elements of Zen training. People who have no particular interest in realization will naturally ask questions if they see you walking strangely, or if they notice your cushions and corner for zazen in your living room. You can keep your mind clear by avoiding superficial conversation about Zen. On the other hand, sincere inquirers can easily be distinguished and encouraged.

The Kyōsaku

In the training center, the monitor carries a flat, narrow stick during periods of zazen. This is the *kyōsaku* (also pronounced *keisaku*), the sword of Manjushri that cuts off concepts and delusions. It is used to strike students on the flat of the shoulders, making a sharp, smacking sound that can be heard throughout the dojo. There is so much misunderstanding about the kyosaku that it deserves careful explanation.

Some writers have reported that the kyosaku is used to awaken students who are asleep and to punish others for wandering thoughts. These are cheap interpretations, with little or no basis in experience. At Ryūtakuji, the monastery where I trained many years ago, I have seen the monitor solemnly pacing the dojo, completely ignoring the bent-over, sleeping forms of fully half the monks in the room. It would be the second day of sesshin, everyone tired and not yet in the full swing of the seven-day seclusion. By the third day there would be a much more alert atmosphere and by the fourth day that same monitor would lightly tap anyone who started to doze off.

As for the kyosaku as punishment, the dojo is not set up that way. When it is used skillfully, the kyosaku is simply a stimulant. Only the shoulder muscles are struck, at such an angle and with the precise force to give a sting, and no more.

In many centers, including our own, the kyosaku is given only when you ask for it. If you feel stale or sleepy, then you may raise your hands in gassho, by way of request, when the monitor walks behind you. As he or she taps your shoulder, return your hands to your lap, tip your head to the left, then to the right, as your shoulders are struck. Afterwards, gassho again. The monitor bows with gassho to you, before and afterwards. This procedure differs slightly from center to center.

The kyosaku is traditionally a "cautionary device," which is the literal meaning of the word. In Far Eastern feudal societies, Zen students were ready for rougher treatment than we in the West would expect. The kyosaku used at our Koko An Zendo in Honolulu is inscribed by Yamada Roshi with a quotation from Yun-men, "I spare you sixty blows."[15] In other words, "What is the use of beating the likes of you!" That's a bigger beating than any blow with a stick, yet those words were a challenge and led to realization for one of Yun-men's students. We in the West have put feudalism behind us, I hope, and few of us could sit still for sixty blows, but these are not signs of weakness. For the rigors of sesshin and for coping with failure, I believe that Western Zen students have grit and determination equal to their Chinese and Japanese ancestors.

The Kyōsaku as a Reminder

The kyosaku is an important reminder to return to the practice. Likewise, when you hear the sound of someone else being struck, you can use that experience as a reminder to come back to your breath counting or back to your koan. When someone coughs, someone moves, someone comes in or goes out, a bird sings outside, a gecko calls, the rain begins or ends, the wind sounds in the trees, your legs hurt—all these sensory experiences can remind you to return to your breath counting.

The Zen training center is not soundproof and in Japan it is completely open to natural elements. When it is cold, it is cold; when it is hot, it is hot. When mosquitoes come, the monks may light mosquito-punk, but the mosquitoes bite anyway. Each little experience of natural happenings can be used as a reminder to stop maundering, stop dreaming, stop fantasizing, stop scheming, stop everything and return to the practice.

Some sounds, however, are penetratingly disturbing. The human voice, even a whisper, perhaps especially a whisper, can shatter one's concentration. Sounds of people moving about carelessly in another room, when you know that *they* know you are doing zazen, can also be disturbing. The TV and radio are disagreeable distractions. The quieter your place is, the better. Then natural sounds will be an actual aid to your practice.

The Kyōsaku Itself

In terms of the practice, the kyosaku and all sense experiences are reminders to return to the theme of your zazen, but fundamentally these sense experiences are full and complete in themselves. Each touch, each sound, each branch you see waving in the wind is a full and complete presentation of itself, with nothing missing and nothing left over. There is a trace of implication, of meaning, in the use of an experience as a reminder. But for the Buddha the morning star was just that star in itself. He then could say that all beings and all things are complete in themselves. What is the significance of the call of the gecko? "Chi! Chi! Chi! Chichichichichi!" That is your morning star.

The Next Step

Now I want you to experiment with a different way of counting your breaths. Instead of counting both inhalation and exhalation, just count your exhalations from "one" to "ten." On the inhalations, keep your mind steady and serene.

This means of practice will demonstrate to you the importance of the exhalation. For one thing, you can settle with the exhalation. You may treat it something like a sigh. For another, the exhalation is organically linked with action. Notice how the *kendō* (fencing) teacher shouts as he strikes. The sound is not so important for our purposes. It is the uniting of exhalation and action that is instructive. Probably mental activity too is related to the exhalation. Your mental act is to quiet your thinking and your physical act is to settle your bodily tension as you become intimate with your counting. At first this seems mechanical; soon it will be natural.

CHAPTER FOUR

Delusions and Pitfalls

Everything falls under the law of change,
like a dream, a phantom, a bubble, a shadow,
like dew or a flash of lightning;
you should contemplate like this.[16]

This poem comes at the end of the *Diamond Sūtra,* and refers not only to the brevity of life, but to its very texture at any moment. It is not substantial; in fact, as the *Heart Sūtra* says, it is empty.[17]

Because the Buddhist doctrine of emptiness cannot be understood intellectually, it is widely misunderstood. Some Buddhist scholars are reduced to explaining it simply as the ultimate of impermanence: "When you say 'now' it is already gone." But this is not the ultimate fact.

Emptiness is simply a term we use to express that which has no quality and no age. It is completely void and at the same time altogether potent. You may call it Buddha nature, self-nature, true nature, but such words are only tags or pointers.

Form is emptiness and as the *Heart Sutra* also says, emptiness is form. The infinite emptiness of the universe is the essential nature of our everyday life of operating a store, taking care of the children, paying our bills, and other ordinary activities.

In realizing all this, we understand how we are just bundles of sense perceptions, with the substance of a dream or a bubble on the surface of the sea. The vanity of the usual kind of self-

41

preoccupation becomes clear, and we are freed from selfish concerns in our enjoyment of the universe as it is, and of our own previously unsuspected depths.

The mind is completely at rest. Nothing carries over conceptually or emotionally. In this place of rest, we are not caught up in the kaleidoscope of thoughts, colors, and forms as they appear, so we do not react out of a self-centered position. We are free to apply our humanity appropriately in the context of the moment according to the needs of people, animals, plants, and things about us. We stand on our own two feet and decide, "I will do this; I will not do that." This sense of proportion is called "compassion," a word that originally meant "suffer with others." "I am what is around me," as Wallace Stevens said in an early poem. Thus you may see that enlightenment and love are not two things.

Zazen is the fundamental way of cultivating enlightenment and love. Each breath is emptiness itself; each breath is appropriate. In zazen periods we devote ourselves wholly to our practice. In this crystal-clear situation, we encounter our self-centered delusions in their most obtrusive form, not diluted by the usual conditions of life. By returning to our practice whenever these delusions arise, we train ourselves in choosing what is fundamentally appropriate, and we loosen the grip that delusions have over us.

Classes of Delusion

In this section I would like to describe three general classes of delusion that almost everyone encounters sooner or later in the practice. Do not suppose that the term "delusion" refers to something harmful or sinful. A delusion, in this sense, is simply a distraction from the path of enlightenment and compassion.

1. The Pursuit of Fantasy. The first of the three kinds of delusion that plague us most often is the pursuit of fantasy. Actually, there is a question of who is pursuing whom. The fantasy pursues the student, or at least it often seems that way.

When caught up in this delusion, you plan, scheme, tell yourself stories, or recall something in full detail from the past. The ordinary self is always at the heart of these mental activities. They have their appropriate place in our daily life, but they are out of context while we are sitting at zazen.

It is not an easy task to break this delusion. You will not be successful if you just try to block your thoughts. You are trying to block yourself, you will end by tiring yourself out, and the fantasy will be as feisty as ever. It is important to sit with a mind that is open, as open as the air. When there is a little sound, let that sound go right through. Notice that if you are absorbed in fantasy, you are enclosed in yourself. You don't hear the little sound. If you are counting your breaths with a pure mind, you are completely open.

When you are caught up by the delusion, at that moment the delusion will occupy you completely. But when it fades a little, you will notice that you have been straying, and you will be able to switch back to breath counting or koan work.

The deliberate pursuit of fantasy is the *bête noir* of zazen. You decide, "I will just put my practice aside for a while and think about this other thing." I once knew a man who used the quiet time of zazen to work on his own business problems. Ultimately he gave up coming to meetings. Perhaps he solved all his problems. If you follow such a way, you are forming bad habits, and will some day have to break them if you are to quiet your mind. It is better not to form them in the first place. There is a time to work out your personal, social, or financial concerns, but zazen is not that time.

2. Random Thoughts. The second kind of delusion in zazen is random thoughts. This too may be a creative process during free time, but on your cushions it is a separation from the practice. You drift and dream, carried along by the flow of images, music, memories, and fantasies. You may not be putting energy into these fragments of mental activity and they may have no particular coherence. Often you may find that you are counting your breaths or working on your koan while these thoughts chatter idly in the background. This is dull zazen, and you need consciously to bring yourself to a sharper effort.

When you begin your practice, and perhaps for a long time afterwards, background noise in your mind will be rather a distraction. This can't be helped. Thinking is the function of your brain, and you are not trying to shut that function down. You are trying to invest in the theme of your practice. In so doing, your random thoughts will die down gradually and naturally.

As Yasutani Roshi used to point out, there are people who have done zazen for several years who think that their object is to quiet all thoughts. It is possible to achieve this condition, but hardly desirable. Our creativity would also be quieted, and where would realization come from? We would become zombies, which is certainly not our object. Our object is to become "one," to become "two," and so on through our breath counting sequence. This practice actually sharpens our ability to think clearly and encourages incisive realization.

3. *Makyō*. The third class of delusion is *makyō*, "mysterious vision." This is a deep-dream experience that may involve a dramatic vision, a feeling of bodily distortion, or less commonly a sensation of hearing or smelling something that is not there in objective fact.

Flora Courtois, in her little book, *An American Woman's Experience of Enlightenment*, vividly describes several makyo, one of which will illustrate the phenomenon:

A scene appeared as from an incalculably remote and primitive time. I seemed to be a member of a small family of cave dwellers. There was darkness, a gloomy darkness about our lives and surroundings. In our cave we had found a place of security and protection from what I sensed to be a hostile outside world. Gradually, however, we found within ourselves the courage as a family to venture forth together to seek a brighter, more open place. Now we found ourselves on a great, open light plain which stretched in all directions and where the horizons seemed to beckon to us with untold possibilities.[18]

For Ms. Courtois, this was the turning point in her practice. The others in her family and indeed most of the human race turned back to the cave, leaving her to go on alone.

Not all makyo are this rich in detail, but all of them are vivid. One student told me of a flock of white doves descending into her body. My own most significant makyo placed me in an ancient temple, also of an incalculably remote time. Its stone pillars reached up to a vastly high ceiling. I was seated on the stone floor and tall monks garbed in black robes walked around me in a circle reciting sutras. Like all deep makyo, this experience was accompanied by a strong feeling of encouragement.

Yasutani Roshi points out that certain religions place great importance upon makyo. Visions and heavenly voices are seriously considered to be signs of enlightenment and salvation. Speaking in tongues is a kind of makyo. Astral walking, with all its variants, is elaborate makyo. These phenomena may be of general interest, for they reveal the rich potential of human experience, but they reveal little of the true nature of the one who experiences them.

In Zen, makyo are a sign that you are making progress with your practice. You have passed beyond the superficial stage of thinking this or that. You are no longer in the world of everyday delusion, and you may be encouraged to feel that if you press on earnestly in your practice, you will realize your true nature before long. The Buddha himself had visions of beautiful women, angels, and devils while he was seated under the Bodhi tree. On the other hand, some completely mature students have never had makyo, so it is not a prerequisite to realization. If you do experience it, however, you can recognize that you are walking near your true home and that it is then important to press on with particular diligence.

I have heard some Zen students, who really should know better, describe makyo as something ultimate. In one sense this is true, but please be careful. "God's voice" is the voice of your own psyche in its present place. It may show that you are near, but that is all.

Always relate your makyo to your teacher, but do not try to cultivate them, for they are spontaneous and cannot be summoned up. When they do occur, let them go as you would any other delusion. Each time you return to your practice, you reinforce in your consciousness the importance of training. No matter how interesting and encouraging thoughts or makyo may be, they are self-limited.

Condition

One specific delusion is preoccupation with personal condition. This is an important matter and deserves extended consideration. First of all, we should notice that many of the things that trouble us seem to have their origins in outward circumstances but are really rooted within. An example is the anger expressed by persons suffering from old age or illness.

During sesshin and at a training center at all times, there is a certain amount of tension. Meals are light; sleep is short; the zazen is hard work; and the living conditions are crowded. One feels quite sensitive, almost transparent. Pockets of feeling that are otherwise unnoticed or are covered over suddenly manifest themselves, perhaps with great virulence, and attach themselves to circumstances. You may feel that someone is deliberately trying to annoy you with wiggling or coughing.

You may be deeply suspicious of the monitor and the teacher, convinced that they are unfriendly, or that they think you are hopeless. You may experience violent resentment of the training and the schedule. Or perhaps long repressed anger against relatives may suddenly come forth like a forest fire, consuming all your energy.

It is probably healthy that such feelings rise into consciousness. It may not be possible just to return to counting when you notice them. They may be too powerful, and will overcome your efforts to ignore them. You must deal with them, but how? One way is to go along with them. "My damned mother" then becomes your meditation. That is no good. A better way is to reflect, "I am angry with my mother." Noticing and acknowledging your feelings is a step toward taking responsibility for them, and reflecting, "This anger comes from me." When this acceptance is wholehearted, then it is possible to return to your counting.

Likewise, if you become angry when your neighbor in the dojo is wiggling unconscionably, it will be easy for you to come back to your practice if you reflect on the true source of your anger. Your fellow student is having a hard time with physical pain or mental anguish. Why are you so unsympathetic? Besides, the monitor is undoubtedly noticing the movement too and will caution the restless one at the appropriate time. There is no need for you to worry about it.

Anger is one kind of condition. Bliss is another condition. The sensation of transparency is still another, sleepiness another, and so on. These conditions are only superficial waves of the sea of your mind. They are the context of your practice. When you are angry, have angry zazen. Just continue to count your breaths, just continue to work on your koan, in that blaze of feeling. When you are in blissful condition, have blissful zazen. When you congratulate yourself on your blissful condition, it disappears immediately. It is simply the nature of the shadow that is your environment.

When you are sleepy, have sleepy zazen. Sleepiness is somehow related to deep zazen, for both are times when the cortex is quieter than usual. Makyo may readily appear. The time of falling asleep or waking up may be the time of realization for the mature student. Don't fight it. During periods of zazen, sit with that sleepiness. Each time you nod, bring yourself back, serenely and easily.

You can sometimes break a cycle of condition by washing your face between periods of sitting, or just taking a drink of water. However, sometimes there is nothing much you can do, and perhaps a whole morning or a whole day during sesshin will pass in which a particular condition is especially vivid. But it will go by eventually. Even moderate pain goes away during sesshin as your condition deepens. It is like having a persistent dream in the night: when daylight comes, the dream is no longer there.

Thinking, too, is a condition. Sit in the context of thoughts. Your thoughts are the environment of your zazen, as much as your room and the TV next door. Sit with those thoughts and don't let them master you. Count "one," "two," "three," and all distractions will become unimportant. You are not, fundamentally, seeking "good condition" of quiet, or avoiding "bad condition" of noise.

Commonly, the Zen teacher will encounter questions that reveal a preoccupation with *samādhi,* or quality of meditation. With careful reading of Zen literature in English, you will find teachers who recommend various samadhi devices—breathing in a certain way; centering your mind in the lower abdomen, and so on. Of course, in one respect, zazen itself is a samadhi device, but it must be understood clearly, once and for all, that samadhi is not the full purpose of our practice. It is more accurate to say that our purpose is to respond to Paul Gauguin's questions, "Where do we come from? What are we? Where do we go?" Or to say that zazen is its own purpose.

I think the proper way to respond to most questions about samadhi is to encourage the student to become one with the practice, to breath the count or the koan, to have the count do the counting, to have the koan work on the koan. There is no special way to direct one's muscles in order to do this, except to relax them within correct posture and to permit the belly to hang out naturally. My own experience with Zen training, which extends over thirty years, is that a teacher's emphasis on samadhi is often in inverse proportion to his emphasis on realization.

Pain

Yamada Roshi says, "Pain in the legs is the taste of Zen." Sometimes he adds, looking around at his students with a smile, "I wonder if you know what I mean." Everybody knows. Everybody hurts during sesshin. Pain is a condition that deserves a special section in this chapter.

The first truth enunciated by the Buddha is that life is suffering. Avoidance of suffering leads to worse suffering. It hurts to face the brevity of our lives, and we drink alcohol excessively to avoid that pain, thus causing more pain. It hurts to share, so we create poverty and war to protect our comfortable greed.

It hurts to stretch our legs, but if we avoid that pain, we suffer the pain of not being able to do zazen. Everybody has a different physical makeup and some people can never hope to sit on cushions. This is all right. Sit at the forward edge of your physical endurance and you will be doing true zazen, even though you are sitting in a chair.

Some people will baby themselves. Looking around the dojo, I see people who are old timers in the practice, though young in years, still sitting in seiza as a regular practice or still moving from cushions to chair and back again. In cases of old injuries that won't heal, this is understandable, but where there is physical resistance, there is spiritual resistance.

Of course, Zen practice is not designed to create samurai. It is not designed to create crippled heroes. I once attended a sesshin where the teacher imposed endurance on his students. We sat for periods as long as an hour and forty minutes. Two people suffered nerve damage in their legs. This is outrageous.

Find the Middle Way. Change your position to seiza at the outset of a new period of zazen by way of relief, or move to a chair at such a time. If the pain becomes too much during a period, let your foot down from the half lotus to the Burmese position. But keep pushing yourself a little. If one of your knees does not touch the pad in the half lotus, place a small cushion under it. Make it thin enough so that you will be stretching.

When you feel pain, return to your breath counting, just as you do when you notice you are thinking about something. However, just as anger or emotional pain may be so severe that ignoring it won't work, so physical pain sometimes over- whelms the practice. In such case, experience that pain for awhile. Acknowledge it as your own. Relax into it. When it eases, return to the count.

One of the *pāramitās,* or perfections, is the perfection of pa- tience, or forbearance. All the paramitas—relinquishment, wisdom, and so on—are marks of the Buddha. Buddha nature breathes in and out, but is always at rest. Rest is the essence of patience. Cultivate rest.

The Sick Soul

One further comment on condition relates to what William James called "the sick soul," what San Juan de la Cruz called "the dark night of our soul," and what David the Psalmist called "the valley of the shadow of death." This is the experi- ence of the spiritual desert, where there is no moisture, no sustenance. It is a supreme attack of the "blahs." Nothing seems of any value or purpose. Everything that was meaningful before now seems absurd, pointless. The student feels pessimistic and discouraged.

This condition may simply be chronic pessimism: the student is overcritical of himself or herself, overidealistic about potential attainment, and perhaps perfectionistic in matters of personal purity. Maybe all such negativity has suddenly come to a head. Teachers can then only encourage students to recognize that they are human beings with a certain capacity, just as all the Buddhas and teachers of the past were individuals with their own unique capacities. There is no reason why all cannot fulfill their capacities. But the person—or personality—is the agent of realization. In one sense, attaining realization is a matter of fully appreciating its agent. Self-hate and self-rejection are blind alleys for the Zen student.

On the other hand, the sick soul may be a condition that directly precedes realization—itself a kind of religious experience. It is an unhappy condition, however, and as David implies in the Twenty-third Psalm, it requires a lot of trust and courage to press on. The Christian and Jew put faith in God in this lonely place. Zen students feel even more alone and must plod along just with trust in the zazen process. The sick soul is actually about to be transformed in great death, the step of dying to oneself that is coincident with rebirth in realization. In the desert of the sick soul, it is important to maintain the practice, to let go of the desert, let go of the sick soul. Simply continue in the same way you have pursued your Zen work up to now. As best you can, invest yourself in the practice. Forget yourself in doing breath counting, in becoming one with the koan.

Personal Problems

Preoccupation with personal problems is another kind of delusion that most Zen students have to cope with. Such preoccupation may be dealt with in three ways. First the problems may be ignored. This seems rather simplistic, perhaps, but it is true that if we feed our problems by paying attention to them, they will grow and flourish. Often the problem is just in one's head. I think it was Josh Billings who said, "I'm an old man, and I've had many troubles, most of which never happened." Treat the problem as you would any distraction in your zazen. Pass it by. Unite with your practice and let the problem go away.

However, the problem may be too persistent to ignore. Perhaps you can take practical steps to resolve it. Talk it over with a trusted friend, write the necessary letter, make the necessary phone call, or try working with a book like *Focusing*.[19] Look the problem in the eye and its hidden cause may come forth and surprise you.

Sometimes the problem won't go away when you ignore it, or even when you take practical steps to resolve it. If it interferes seriously with your practice, professional counseling may be required. I hope the counselor can be one who sympathizes with the zazen process. Perhaps this psychological work can run in tandem with zazen. Maybe the zazen will have to stop for a while.

Self-Doubt

Perfectionism may evoke the question, "Am I sincere enough to do zazen?" When asked about sincerity, Yasutani Roshi said, "Five-percent sincerity is enough to begin with. If you were completely sincere, you would be enlightened at this moment." Sincerity builds, like everything else in our practice. There is no use blaming ourselves for being human.

Sometimes you may feel that your zazen is worse than it was a few months earlier. This may be true; zazen is a zigzag path, but only when judged by samadhi terms of a quiet mind or a concentration of spirit. You can be confident that you are ripening all the while. However, it is more likely that your memory is playing tricks on you. The enthusiasm that you felt at the outset of your practice has worn away and you are left with the reality of difficult training. Or you may be more sensitive to distractions and the noisy mind you hardly noticed before is all too distracting now. This kind of concern is just another preoccupation with condition. Wipe it away and return to your practice.

Zazen for Married People

If one spouse is not interested in zazen or any sort of meditation practice, both partners must exercise particular care not to allow it to become an instrument of division. Especially in the United States, where husband and wife will even wear matching clothes and seek to integrate many of their activities, any separation into something that requires personal investment can be a threat. When only one partner is interested in Zen, he or she may have to give up quite a bit of zazen time for family activities.

The uninterested spouse must not feel pushed into something that seems a violation of deeply held convictions. Humanist, Jewish, or Christian doctrines may seem at first to be violated by Zen practice. It may take months, or even years, to learn that this is not so. The husbands and wives who come around to zazen after a while will be those who are convinced by the changes in their spouse, not by coercion.

Spouses who are not interested in zazen should be made welcome at all Sangha socials and outings. These socials will demonstrate that the teacher and other students are not so peculiar after all, and doubts and fears may be eased.

Children

Children may wish to copy their parents and do zazen with them. In Japan, parents have learned not to encourage this. Children are taught how to gassho and bow before the altar, and are read stories of the Buddha. But at zazen time they are either asleep or they are sent out to play. The rationale is that there can be no fundamental interest in zazen until after puberty. If the child shows interest, it will only be for brief periods. Sitting as long as twenty-five minutes may set up resistance that can block interest in the practice later on.

So if your children show interest, explain that they may sit with you if they wish but that they should not feel any compulsion. Tell them that they may come in and sit at any time, and leave at any time. Make a game afterwards of having them tell what they thought about. If they ask you about your practice, tell them about breath counting, but don't make a big point of it. They should feel that they can try it or not, as they like. If they choose not to sit at all, show them special attention after you have finished, so that they will feel all right about not doing it. Children too should be made welcome at Sangha socials and outings.

Children love ritual, so in addition to teaching them to gassho and to offer incense and flowers, their religious education can include a brief *gāthā* before the meal, such as:

> We venerate the Three Treasures
> and are thankful for this meal,
> the work of many people
> and the sharing of other forms of life.[20]

The Three Treasures are discussed in Chapter Six.

The Next Step

I would like to have you experiment now with a new way of counting your breaths. You have been counting exhalations, keeping your mind steady and silent on the inhalations. Try reversing this process. Count the inhalations only and keep your mind silent on the exhalation. This is less natural, as your mental and physical actions are generally geared to exhalations, but it will give you a new slant on meditative concentration. You inhale for half your life, after all. Take in "one," take in "two," and so on, up to "ten."

CHAPTER FIVE

Attitudes in
Religious Practice

The word "Zen" is the Japanese pronunciation of the Chinese *ch'an,* which is in turn an abbreviation of *ch'an-na,* the closest Chinese could come to saying *dhyāna,* the Sanskrit word meaning meditation. So we may say, Zen means meditation and the Way of Zen is the Way of Meditation. In this sense, Zen would be quite free of any sectarian limitation.

In his "Introductory Lectures," Harada Roshi cited the classical "Five Types of Zen," and his successors have followed his example. However, this catalog has an arbitrary quality common to many prescientific classification systems, and includes errors of type. That is, the types set forth are not sufficiently exclusive of each other to be separate in category. Indeed, one of the types is simply everything non-Buddhist, a wastebasket category too blurred to be useful.

Moreover, while Harada Roshi sought to show that Zen is not limited to a certain Japanese-Chinese-Indian tradition, still the broad use of Zen to designate the way of, say, Ramana Maharshi or Inayat Khan seems just too presumptuous. If we use the word "Zen" to describe the teachings of such masters, we will seem, at least, to be tarring everybody with our own brush.

So with all respect to my teachers, I will set aside "Types of Zen" and instead try to say something about attitudes found generally in religious practice. My purpose, as always, is to present Zen as one option among many and if ever I seem to be making invidious comparisons, it will be out of ignorance of other paths, not because I want to show Zen in such a shining light.

The Humanist Attitude

First, I wish to take up the attitude that may best be described as humanist. It is religious, as it guides people in a way of life, but it has no connection with formal religion. An example would be *Seiza Shiki,* "The System of Quiet Sitting." I described seiza in chapter two as the posture of sitting on a cushion with the legs doubled back so that the feet are on each side of the seat. This position has its source in the ordinary way of sitting on the *tatami* in Japan; in fact, another name for seiza is *Nihon-za,* or "Japanese sitting." In the Seiza Shiki, people sit in Japanese fashion on a pad, but without a cushion, with their feet tucked under their bottoms. Groups of people meet to practice seiza together in cities and towns all over Japan. You also see people in trains, buses, and waiting rooms sitting quietly with their eyes lowered and their faces serene. In Seiza Shiki, people are advised to slow down their exhalations and to focus on their breathing, centering themselves in the lower abdomen. They sit and sit, and say it is very good for their health.

Seiza is the position taken in various arts of Japan—calligraphy, tea ceremony, flower arrangement, and so on. In fact, zazen itself is taught as a corollary art in some tea ceremony academies. Many teachers of such martial arts as *karate* and *aikido* will have their students sit in seiza or actually in the lotus position for a while before working out in the gym. The idea seems to be that if the students quiet their minds they will strengthen their *ki,* or spirit, the vital element of such martial activities.

The Japanese army has long used seiza for disciplining purposes, much as a mother in Western countries might have her child sit in the corner if he or she becomes unruly. In recent years, Japanese penologists have developed a system of character correction, using seiza with assigned themes of filial piety.

In my limited experience in Zen Buddhist monasteries in Japan, I have known monks who shaved their heads and took vows for a variety of humanist reasons that could only be called therapeutic. I knew a monk who sought to cure his asthma, another who sought to correct a tendency toward kleptomania, and one who was a calligraphy teacher dissatisfied with the character revealed by his own calligraphy. The last individual left his family and career and trained as a monk for eight years at Ryutaku Monastery in Mishima. When he was satisfied that he was mature, he returned to his family and his high school teaching position.

Well, only in Japan. In the West, people come to Zen with many different attitudes and purposes, many of them not overtly religious. The humanist-religious distinction is basically false: a more accurate distinction would be "shallow-deep," and none of us start out very deep in the practice anyway.

The Eschatological Attitude

Eschatology deals with death and with life thereafter. The eschatological attitude is concerned with future time and with the practice necessary to ensure that the future time will be rewarding. Depending on the tradition, future time may extend endlessly, life after life.

I once met a Tibetan Buddhist teacher who had just arrived in the West. He had heard about Zen and was full of questions about it. "What kind of visualization exercises do you practice in Zen?" he asked.

I explained that in Zen meditation, we begin with breath counting and then, if appropriate, go on to koan study. "What is a koan?" he asked.

I said, "When the Buddha was enlightened, he exclaimed, 'Now I see that all beings are the Tathagata.' What did he mean?"

"He meant that all beings have the seed of Buddhahood."[21]

Having the seed of Buddhahood is not the same as being Buddha from the beginning. In the Tibetan tradition of this teacher, one cultivates the *development* of Buddhahood. In Zen, we practice to realize what has always been true. We wipe away concepts and hang-ups, delusions and attachments, but as Hakuin Zenji says, "Nirvana is right here, before our eyes."[22] Both paths require time and effort, but the attitudes and purposes are very different.

Another example of the eschatological attitude may be found in the teachings of Jōdō Shinshū, one of the streams of Pure Land Buddhism in Japan. The usual Shinshu follower chants veneration to Amitābha Buddha, the Buddha of Infinite Light and Life, *"Namu Amida Butsu,"* believing that Amida, or Amitabha, will thereby bring the follower to the Pure Land after death. Many Christians may see similarities here to their own way.

The Arhat Ideal

In South and Southeast Asian Buddhism, the *Arhat* is the ultimate human ideal, the enlightened hermit, who in Wumen's words, "Walks the universe alone."[23] This state illustrates one aspect of deepest experience:

> A monk asked Pai-chang Huai-hai, "What is a matter of special wonder?"
> Pai-chang said, "Sitting alone at Ta Hsiung Peak."[24]

Ta Hsiung Peak was the location of Pai-chang's monastery. Yasutani Roshi points out in his commentary on this story that Pai-chang was always alone. He walked alone; he ate alone; he laughed alone. In contrast, the other aspect of deepest experience is complete unity with the whole universe as presented by the Bodhisattva, the ideal of Northern Buddhism, who sacrifices his or her own enlightenment for the sake of others. Pai-chang expressed his Bodhisattva spirit also, by his instructive reply to the monk, a reply that may enlighten us all.

We must not confuse the position of the Arhat with ordinary delusion. Of course the Arhat knows that he or she is one with everything. His or her position is just one part of the truth, as the Bodhisattva's position is the other part. Fundamentally, the two aspects are one, not even one.

Ordinary delusion is the position of self-centeredness, where I am using you. The industrialist says, "I can use that person." The employee says, "I can use this company." And so the system is perpetuated. The inquirer at a training center may say, "I want to find a good place to do zazen." This is a natural, innocent statement, but it expresses a self-centered concern. With a certain amount of training, however, that individual may say, "I want to help make this a good place to do zazen."

Buddhism that idealizes the Arhat, the Buddhism of Sri Lanka, of Burma, Thailand, and of other Southeast Asian countries, has been called *Hīnayāna,* or "Lesser Vehicle." The doctrine has been misunderstood to mean that you must be concerned with just your own emancipation. This idea is then contrasted with *Mahāyāna,* or "Great Vehicle," where people are concerned with the emancipation of everyone in the universe. These invidious terms were invented by Mahayana people, who illustrate thereby the meanness of bragging about your own generosity.

As we have seen, the Arhat knows very well that he or she is one with everything. This point is realized in Southern Buddhist countries, in Sri Lanka, for example, where two of the main universities of the country are run entirely by Buddhist monks. Orphanages and hospitals are also Buddhist. Sarvodaya Shramadana, a nation-wide village development movement, is based on Buddhist principles. Similar Buddhist movements are found in Thailand, while in Japan, a Mahayana country, Buddhist social welfare programs are almost nonexistent, Buddhist universities are generally weak except in their special sectarian fields, and social action by traditional Buddhists seems confined to defensive statements designed to protect sectarian status. Notable exceptions are subsects of Nichiren Buddhism, such as the Nichihonzan Myōhōji, which are active in movements for peace and social justice.

The terms Hinayana and Mahayana are convenient to scholars, just as certain inherently sexist terms are convenient to writers of English. It is important that we discipline ourselves to avoid invidious terminology and at the same time remain faithful to the demands of rhetoric and truth.

The Bodhisattva Ideal

Although the Bodhisattva ideal has been a doctrinal development in Northern Buddhism, in fact, the life of devotion to the welfare of others has not been a sectarian phenomenon in world history. Mother Teresa, Mahatma Gandhi, A. T. Ariyaratne—Bodhisattvas emerge in all religious and cultural lines. My first teacher, Senzaki Nyogen *Sensei,* used to address us as "Bodhisattvas," the way another speaker might say, "Ladies and Gentlemen." He was not downgrading the term, but appealing to the Bodhisattva-nature of each of us.

There would be no American Zen as we know it today, including no Diamond Sangha, if it were not for Senzaki Sensei, who lived quietly with a small group of students, first in San Francisco, then in Los Angeles, for more than fifty years in the early part of this century. Senzaki Sensei gave his life fully to all of us. He was a true Bodhisattva and there were countless Bodhisattvas before him, all of them devoting all their energy to us. Unless we too develop as Bodhisattvas, there will be no

Buddha Dharma here and now—it will only be a memory set forth superficially in books in time to come.

The universe is one. How can you be enlightened unless all others are enlightened too? St. Paul said, "The whole creation groaneth and travaileth in pain together until now." The word "travail" means the labor of childbirth. We are all of us involved in the great labor of the universe. This is the path we set forth in our vows:

> Though the many beings are numberless,
>   I vow to save them;
> though greed, hatred, and ignorance rise endlessly,
>   I vow to cut them off;
> though the Dharma is vast and fathomless;
>   I vow to understand it;
> though Buddha's way is beyond attainment;
>   I vow to embody it fully. [25]

I have heard people say, "I cannot recite these vows because I cannot hope to fulfill them." Actually, Kanzeon, the incarnation of mercy and compassion, weeps because she cannot save all beings. Nobody fulfills these "Great Vows for All," but we vow to fulfill them as best we can. They are our path.

When we start out, we may be preoccupied with personal problems, the attitudes of others toward ourselves, and by personal ambition for religious experience and leadership. But as our training continues, our motivation may deepen, and we can put aside such personal concerns and exert ourselves with our sisters and brothers.

As the world is going, the Bodhisattva ideal holds our only hope for survival or indeed for the survival of any species. The three poisons of greed, hatred and ignorance are destroying our natural and cultural heritage. I believe that unless we as citizens of the world can take the radical Bodhisattva position, we will not even die with integrity.

Inherent Completion

The attitude that all is complete from the very beginning fulfills the ideals of the Arhat and the Bodhisattva. It is a realization that the essential world of perfection is this very world of gain and loss, birth and death, cause and effect. We practice as Arhats or Bodhisattvas to realize what has always been true. When Dogen Zenji said, "Zazen is itself enlightenment," he was speaking from this fundamental standpoint.

Counting our breaths, we practice the inherent completion of all things. That "one" is the full presentation of the whole universe. That "two" likewise is the full presentation of the whole universe. And so on, for each point in the sequence.

Each step on the road is the Tathagata coming forth. With each step, you are the Bodhisattva Kanzeon, with eleven heads and a thousand arms, saving all beings. Someone asked the Korean Zen teacher, Seung Sahn, "How can I save all beings?" He replied, "They are already saved." Our "Great Vows for All" are already fulfilled.

The music of Mozart is already heavenly. We play it, awkwardly at first, then better and better. But each note stands forth, full and complete in its perfection.

Likewise, in counting our breaths, idle thoughts take us away and we return again and again to "one." What is that act of return but the full and complete point of "one"? Here you may be very clever and ask, "But isn't dreaming of seduction full and complete?" Of course it is! Nothing missing! Nothing left over! By all means, sit there and continue to dream of seduction. You will be consistent in philosophy. But I want to be consistent in practice.

Zen practice is not the only way of inherent completion. Within the Jodo Shinshu tradition are the *Myōkōnin,* the "Subtly Pure People," who realize with the recitation of "Namu Amida Butsu" that they are not merely assured of rebirth in the Pure Land when they die, but that the Pure Land is the ground upon which they stand and Amitabha is their own being—a direct echo of Hakuin Zenji in his "Song of Zazen":

> This very place is the Lotus Land;
> this very body, the Buddha.[26]

We find teachings of heaven as the here and now in some Western and Near Eastern traditions, as well as in Zen Buddhism. These are the dark, or inner, or gnostic teachings, sometimes even banned by orthodox eschatologists. They persist, however; we find that the sermons of Meister Eckhart and the poetry of Rumi and Kabir resonate with the words of Hakuin Zenji.

There are problems with the eschatological attitude. There may be tendencies to be preoccupied with sin and human faults and to postpone realization to some future time of perfection.

There are problems with Hakuin Zenji's words also. There may be a tendency to overlook personal failings and to take an antinomian position: "I am enlightened, so I may do as I wish." Of the two sets of problems, I find the arrogance of presumed spiritual attainment to be the most pernicious. I relate much more easily to the humble religious, laboring in the fields by day, and caught up in prayer by night, never doubting that the glory of God awaits.

Kinds of Zen Buddhism

Attitudes in religious practice devolve naturally into sectarian paths. Within Japanese Zen these are three; Rinzai, Sōtō, and Ōbaku. Rinzai and Soto were introduced into Japan in the late twelfth and thirteenth centuries; the Obaku is a reintroduction of the Rinzai school after it had mixed in China with

Amitabha pietism. The Obaku school is rather small and isolated from the two larger streams.

Both Rinzai and Soto declined gradually over the centuries after flourishing in the Kamakura Period and shortly thereafter. Hakuin Zenji reorganized and revitalized the Rinzai school in the eighteenth century and today all Rinzai Zen teachers trace their lineage through him, while all other lines of Rinzai Zen have died out. Although the Rinzai school has declined again in the past hundred years and some of its main temples function today largely as museums, it nonetheless still thrives in many monasteries in our own time.

Soto Zen was founded in Japan by Dogen Zenji, a teacher of towering importance in Buddhism generally, as well as within his own tradition of Zen. Since his time, however, we can trace a steady decline over the centuries. Exceptional teachers, such as the late Suzuki Shunryū Roshi of the San Francisco Zen Center, still appear, and one finds among long-time Soto Zen students a modesty of character that rises from the practice of *shikantaza,* or "pure sitting." Modern Soto Zen does not use koan study and seldom mentions realization. Instead the emphasis is on just-sitting, mindfulness, and serving others.

Sanbō Kyōdan

In the early years of this century, Soto monks in search of Zen training were disappointed to find it generally unavailable in their school. Such monks as Watanabe Genshū, Kohō Chisan, and Harada Daiun studied with Rinzai teachers, Watanabe and Koho with Miyagi Sokai Zenji and Shaku Soen Zenji in Kamakura, respectively, and Harada with Toyota Dokutan Zenji in Kyoto. All three of these monks returned to the Soto fold after completing their Rinzai training, but only Harada Roshi took steps to reorganize the training within his monastery to use koans in the practice.

Harada Roshi's course of zazen training for students interested in realizing self-nature usually begins with the koan *Mu*, though sometimes another preliminary koan may be used. This is followed by a series of selected koans designed to establish a perspective for the practice, and then four anthologies of koans—two books that are generally associated with the Rinzai school and two with the Soto. A fifth collection provides recapitulation of insights established in koan study and the realization of the essential ground of Buddhist precepts.

The line of teachers Harada, Yasutani Hakuun, and Yamada Kōun has emerged as a lay movement, known as the *Sanbō Kyōdan*, or "Order of the Three Treasures." It is an independent sect of Zen Buddhism intended as a revitalization of the line of Dogen Zenji. Its headquarters is in Kamakura at the *Sanun Zendo*. Other centers are located in Hokkaido, Osaka, Wakayama Prefecture, Kyushu, Munich, Hawaii, and Manila.

The Diamond Sangha is the Hawaii center. It in turn has associated centers in Sydney, Australia (The Sydney Zendo) and Nevada City, California (The Ring of Bone Zendo). The Zen Center of Los Angeles is connected with the Sanbo Kyodan through its teacher, Maezumi Hakuyū Roshi, who was a disciple of Yasutani Roshi and who also holds transmission from traditional Rinzai and Soto lines.

The Next Step

Now I should like you to try still another way of meditation. Don't count; just follow your breaths, inhale, exhale. Let all of your thoughts go by until there is just the breath. As Suzuki Shunryu Roshi used to say, it is like a door swinging in the wind, nothing comes in, nothing goes out.

CHAPTER SIX

The Three Treasures

The three Treasures are the Buddha, the Dharma, and the Sangha. The ceremony acknowledging them as our home is central to the religious life of the Zen Buddhist, in much the same way that Holy Communion is central to the religious life of the Catholic Christian. This is the *Ti Saraṇa Gamana,* or "Taking the Three Refuges," and is important for all Buddhists, not only Zen students. You will find this ceremony in every temple of Buddhism, in South and Southeast Asia, in the diaspora of Tibetan Buddhism, in Taiwan and Hong Kong, and in Korea and Japan.

The Buddha

The first treasure is the Buddha. This refers, of course, to Shakyamuni, the historical founder of Buddhism, but it also has a far broader meaning. It includes mythological personages who preceded Shakyamuni and dozens of archetypical figures in the Buddhist pantheon. It includes all the great teachers of our lineage—Bodhidharma, Hui-nêng, Ma-tsu, Pai-chang, Chao-chou, Yun-men, down through such Japanese worthies as Dogen and Hakuin to our own teachers. It includes not only such outstanding figures, but also everyone who has realized his or her nature—all the hundreds of thousands of monks, nuns, and lay people in Buddhist history who have shaken the tree of life and death.

In a deeper and yet more ordinary dimension, all of us are Buddha. We haven't realized it yet, perhaps, but that does not deny the fact. Shakyamuni exclaimed, "All beings of the universe are the Tathagata." Buddhist pronouncements are often lofty, but their scope includes the humble realms of worms and nettles. The whole universe is enlightenment.

The human being at this stage in world evolution has a chance to realize the Tathagata. This is a wonderful opportunity, but it means simply that we can realize things as they are.

When Hakuin Zenji wrote in his "Song of Zazen," "All beings by nature are Buddha," he used the Japanese translation of the word "Buddha"—*Hotoke*. There is also the Japanese term *Butsu*, which is a transliteration of "Buddha" and which has particular technical or sectarian references. Hotoke means Buddha, but also something close to the Western word "gods," as in the Greek or Roman pantheons. Shibayama Zenkei Roshi points out in his *A Flower Does Not Talk* that Hakuin Zenji was radical in his statement, for by using Hotoke instead of Butsu or one of the compounds using Butsu, he was also saying, in effect, all beings by nature are gods.[27] Lofty indeed!

While all beings are indeed the Tathagata, the highest and best, announcing this, even thinking it, can be a kind of delusion. The realized person knows about it, but is not attached to such delusive words as "Buddhahood." Thus the words of the ordinary person and the realized person may often be the same.

There is a folk saying in Japan, "The ordinary person is the Buddha." Indeed, Nan-ch'üan P'u-yüan, one of the great T'ang period worthies, said, "Ordinary mind is the way."[28] Most Zen people carry on apparently unexceptional lives and avoid setting themselves apart by sprinkling their conversations with special Zen words, or by behaving in any kind of exclusive manner. They do not put on a wise or pious act. Yet they realize that all things, including themselves, are totally empty and at the same time charged with energy. This realization is Buddha. It takes hard practice.

The Dharma

The second treasure is the Dharma. It is the vast and fathomless universe: void on the one hand, full and complete on the other. These two aspects are set forth just for purposes of explication. In reality, the Dharma is at once empty and overflowing with beings and things.

From potent emptiness, as potent emptiness, come forth riches, the elements of our universe. Thus, another meaning of Dharma is "phenomena." Even thoughts and the facts we deduce about our world are Dharma.

The Buddha Dharma is Buddhist teaching about the universe. Thousands of books and millions of words make up the Dharma in this sense. It also means "the truth of Buddhism." We say that when Shakyamuni preached, he turned the wheel of the Dharma.

So Dharma is the way, and indeed it is often translated into Chinese as "tao." Tao is a term with a richness of its own. The basic book of Taoism, the *Tao Te Ching,* says, "The way which can be followed is not the true way."[29] We do not follow the Buddha, we practice the way he uncovered, we do the Dharma.

The word "Dharma" is written with the ideograph for "law" in Chinese and Japanese, which is etymologically faithful to the original Sanskrit. By this we can understand the implications of Dharma as the law of the universe, the way things are, the way they behave. For the Buddhist, there is no difference between the Buddha Dharma and ordinary Dharma. Both are Dharma, now expounded by a Buddhist teacher, now by an astronomer or a poet, now by a stone or a bird.

Expressed most simply, the way things behave is that they move. In fact, we can say that things and facts are no more than their behavior, always acting and reacting with all other things. The stone sits in the earth, and any static quality is only in the eye of the impatient human observer, for it is steadily acting and reacting with soil, wind, sunshine, and rain. Phenomena are not nouns, but verbs. Everything is actively manifesting the law of the universe and of individual being. What is the law? It is action and the inevitability of its consequences. What I say here may not be so profound or important, but it will reverberate through all time like a perfectly made bell, creating change upon change.

This is *karma,* the action of Dharma. Karma is understood in a superstitious way by many people to mean that willy-nilly I must pay for all the bad actions I have taken in the past, including past lives. This would be true if I were some kind of automaton, responding by preset controls to my environment. Such a view of karma ignores the nature of the individual, coming forth as essential nature. You and I interact with each incident of the moment. All phenomena of past, present, and future are involved, and the individual action is a creative presentation of the universe.

With our delusions and attachments, we may not be able to act from our empty, potent nature. Attachment, as the Buddha used that term, is a blind response to some action in the past. If I am hit, I hit back. If my parents beat me, then I beat my children. "Freedom from karma" is not some miraculous wiping away of one's past, but rather freedom from blind response to it. If I am hit, I need not hit back. I can evoke from the universe the appropriate response because my mind is calm and empty. The *Chêng Tao Ko* says:

> When awakened we find karmic hindrances fundamentally
> empty,
> but when not awakened, we must repay all our debts.[30]

This does not, of course, mean that I must wait until I am fully enlightened before I can be free from blind response, and neither does it mean that I need not apologize for being rude just because I do zazen. It means that intrinsically I am not burdened by the grief and anguish I have created in the world. I acknowledge that grief and anguish and my responsibility for it, not only to myself, but openly to everyone. At the beginning of the Diamond Sangha sutra service, we recite the "Purification Gatha":

All the evil karma ever created by me since of old,
on account of my beginningless greed, hatred, and
    ignorance,
born of my body, mouth, and thought,
I now confess, openly and fully.[31]

This gatha presents a problem for some people that is similar to their difficulty with the "Great Vows for All." How can I confess to all that garbage I have created in just four simple lines? I can't. But this confession evokes the mind that is neither stained nor pure, and is always at rest.

Blind reaction is not possible when this gatha is repeated from your heart. In Buddhist literature we find many stories of horrible crimes that with the earnest practice of their perpetrators became empty of karmic hindrance to realization and a peaceful mind.

One more point about karma: it is only a word. Once I heard someone say, "I am here because of the Law of Karma." This is not so. The apple did not fall beside Newton because of the Law of Gravity. The law is just something we say about the phenomenon. Many people blame something they call karma for their misfortunes.

Understanding that karma is just a word helps us to understand that there is no such thing as separate cause and effect. Everything is a cause. Everything is an effect. Chu-chih's act of raising one finger was a full and complete act, with no past or future. Yet it also came from the vast reaches of past time and will extend into the inconceivable reaches of future time.

Is your present reading of this book an effect? Yes, it is the result of 84,000 influences. Is it a cause? Yes, for better or for worse. Is it full and complete in itself? Yes, but perhaps it is a pity to say so right out.

Our zazen is like that—full and complete with each breath. Each breath has nothing missing, nothing left over. But there is also progression; gradually your practice becomes purer until you can see into your true nature. Finally you can integrate your realization into everyday life and all traces of enlightenment as a special thing will disappear. This is the karmic, step-by-step aspect of zazen.

So karma may be understood as a word that is descriptive of the Dharma and Dharma may be seen as a word of infinite implications. Basically, the Dharma is pure and clear essential nature itself. And it comes forth as the form of that infinite emptiness. As the *Heart Sutra* says, "Emptiness is no other than form . . . emptiness is exactly form."[32] The Buddha's teaching, the Law of Karma, and phenomena themselves—all are jewels of empty infinity, infinite emptiness. David the Psalmist expressed this in his way:

> The heavens declare the glory of God
> and the firmament showeth his handiwork.

The Sangha

Originally, "Sangha," from a Sanskrit root meaning "an aggregate," referred to the disciples of the historical Buddha. Later it came to mean "priesthood," as the religion of Buddhism got started. In some streams of modern Buddhism, the word still refers only to monks and nuns as a group, but in Zen the Sangha has always been more than clergy, more than a group of believers, more than just Buddhists. The Sangha is, in fact, the kinship of all things, every entity of this universe and of all universes, past, present, and future, in endless dimensions. It is to the enlightenment of this total Sangha that we are dedicated in our vows.

Once Anne Aitken and I were showing Nakagawa Roshi

around the Ojai Valley, in California. Viewing a grassy hillside that had many boulders jutting from its surface, he cried out, "How many members are here!" Each boulder is a member, each tree, each mouse, each intestinal worm.

Once, someone asked me, "What is a being?" I replied, "A quadratic equation." Later he returned and asked, "How can I save a quadratic equation?" I replied, "By including it."

We save all beings by including them. The Sixth Great Ancestor, Hui-neng, explained the first of the Great Vows as, "Though the many beings are numberless, I vow to save them in my own mind."[33]

My mind and yours already include all beings. They are already saved. Our task as a Sangha is to realize that fact in our hearts and in all hearts.

There are many Sanghas within the universal Sangha. The Buddha Sangha is one. This is the kinship of all Buddhists. The Zen Buddhist Sangha is another. The immediate Sangha of the training center is still another. It is from the family that we move into the world. It is from the training center family that we cultivate a larger garden.

At the training center, we have a choice among organizational options. Our model is the Net of Indra—each knot is an individual person, altogether his or her own jewel and not like any other. At the same time, each is a reflection of every other jewel. If we pool all our money, time, and energy, we are neglecting the individual. If we just agree to live in the same house with each person acting independently, then we are neglecting the community. Some money must be contributed to the temple program, some must be held for personal use. Some time and energy goes into a common schedule, some must be free for individual concerns. Working all this out requires flexibility and compassion, and the final guidelines should be clear.

Using a particular style, we risk becoming sectarian. The three poisons of greed, hatred, and ignorance may then be our guide and we may tend to become as exclusive as any class, race, or nationality. Our whole world is in danger because nations cannot surmount nationalism. Some people ask me why I conduct sesshin periodically for Christians. I reply, "To help them to become better Christians," but I don't always get my point across.

To tell another story about Nakagawa Roshi: Once Anne and I were in his mother's cottage at Ryutakuji, listening to a recording of Gregorian chants. Before he put on the record, the Roshi explained to his attendant monk, "This is the way Western monks recite their sutras." Underlying his words was an acknowledgment that East is East and West is West; we have our Sangha and they have their Sangha; but we all of us come forth in our practice to present essential nature to all beings. We are all of us one Sangha. Or, as Nakagawa Roshi expressed it on another occasion, "We are all members of the same nose-hole society."

Finally, it is important to acknowledge the Sangha as the harmony of Buddha and Dharma. Infinite emptiness, full of potential, has its form in phenomena, as they come and go. This is the fundamental truth of Buddhism, "Form is emptiness; emptiness is form," which modern physics, in its complicated way, is coming to understand. The Sangha is our realization of this harmony, this oneness, the undifferentiated vigor of the unknown and unknowable and its expression as the song of the Chinese thrush. We are, you and I, the Tathagata, showing that harmony in each of our actions, standing up, putting on clothes, sitting down for a meal. All fellowship, all ordinary meaning of Sangha spirit, rises from this intimacy.

The Three Refuges

At the beginning of our sutra services, we chant in Pali the "Ti Sarana Gamana":

Buddham saranam gacchāmi;
Dhammam saranam gacchāmi;
Sangham saranam gacchāmi. [34]

In using the liturgical language of Southern Buddhism for this gatha, we follow the example of Senzaki Nyogen Sensei, who sought always to show that Buddhism is a single stream and not divided into separate sects.

Usually the "Ti Sarana" is translated:

I take refuge in the Buddha;
I take refuge in the Dharma;
I take refuge in the Sangha.

This may be the best translation when all is said and done, but it is important to examine the Pali words closely so that we may appreciate the levels of meaning that are not brought out in the English.

The first words in each of the three lines are inflected forms of Buddha, Dharma, and Sangha. "Saranam" is an inflected form of "sarana" which means "protection, shelter, abode, refuge, willed or chosen resort." "Gacchami" is a verb form meaning "going to" or "will undertake." Thus a translation of the first line of the "Ti Sarana" would be, "I undertake to find my home in the Buddha," and the three lines are thus more of a vow than a prayer. The implication is that by finding my home in Buddha, Dharma, and Sangha I can free myself from blind conditioning and realize true nature. Placed at the beginning of the service at the start of a day of zazen, the "Ti Sarana" is a renewal of devotion to the way of enlightenment, practice, and compassion.

In Sino-Japanese, "Saranam gacchami" is translated *kie,* which means "to turn to and rely upon." *Ki,* or return, also means "come down to, result in, belong to." This translation makes it clear that the Buddha, Dharma, and Sangha are already my home, and I am devoted to them. With them as my abode, I am freed from cycles of karma that bind me to repetitive action and reaction.

To realize the very heart of essential nature is to take refuge in the Buddha. To cultivate the garden of realization is to take refuge in the Dharma. To share the fruits of the garden is to take refuge in the Sangha. Yasutani Roshi says, "The 'Ti Sarana Gamana' is the foundation and the whole of the Buddha Tao."[35]

The Three Treasures at the Training Center

Fundamentally, everything is enlightened from the beginning, and our task at the Zen training center is to realize that fact ever more deeply and clearly. Hakuin Zenji says in his "Song of Zazen" that the paramitas (relinquishment, virtuous conduct, forbearance, zeal, meditative concentration, and wisdom) all find their home in zazen. As I indicated earlier, paramita means "perfection," implying the realization of Buddhahood. We realize Buddhahood through deep zazen and through personal interviews, Dharma talks, classes in the doctrine, reading, social interaction, maintenance work, and all aspects of living at our training center and in our homes. Thus we find our home in the Buddha.

Some people come to the training center for meetings and for sesshin. Others may live at the center and either stay there full-time for zazen and maintenance work, or go out to work or to college during the day, devoting evenings and early mornings to zazen. But whether you are a community member or a resident of the training center, you can join with your sisters and brothers in cultivating each moment as a Dharma treasure.

In the *"Enmei Jikku Kannon Gyō* (Ten Verse Kanzeon Sutra of Eternal Life)," we recite *"Nen nen ju shin ki/Nen nen fu ri shin."*

"Thought after thought arises in the mind;/Thought after thought is not separate from mind."[36] "Thought after thought" is the very nature of our mind. When this "thought after thought" is harmoniously working together with other people, animals, plants, and things, we are united with the task at hand and with moving from one task to another. We are united with the Dharma of our day. We give energy to this Dharma; we channel energy to it from unknown wellsprings. We find our home in the Dharma and join in the world's work.

Yasutani Roshi used to say, "The fundamental delusion of humanity is to suppose I am here and you are out there." He would point to himself with "here" and to his listeners with "out there," miming the division conceived by self-centered people. It is by living together at the training center, or at home and training at the center with residents, that we learn to correct such self-preoccupation. Of course the workaday world provides ample opportunity to correct such ignorance also, but underlying our acquisitive society is the dirty secret that we conspire to work along with each other's greed in order to further our own. Most situations in the workaday world require by unwritten ideology and by clear example that we not be too concerned about others. Our lives in the larger community are in loving resistance to such self-centered attitudes.

At the Zen training center, and at other religious centers and humanist communities as well, an ideology is clearly set forth in writing and by example to counter the greed, hatred, and ignorance that is all around. We realize truly that we form a single organism with all beings and with all inanimate things of the universe. Together we enrich this realization individually, and as a fellowship, among ourselves, among our neighbors, and in the world. Thus we find our home in the Sangha.

The Next Step

Now I want you to experiment with still another way of zazen. This is shikantaza, or pure sitting. It is a mature way of sitting, generally only for the most experienced student. However, it is important for all students to have a sense of what it is. Moreover, there are some people for whom shikantaza is the best way from the beginning of their practice.

After you have counted your breaths for one or two sequences, just sit facing the empty stage of your mind. Settle into your bones and guts. There are no thoughts, no numbers, and no themes at all. Give it your best try for a few periods of practice, at least.

CHAPTER SEVEN

The Ten
Grave Precepts

Fellowship at the Zen Center is the microcosm of the fellowship of all beings, all inanimate things, and all unseen elements of unknown dimensions. A deep sense of the Sangha is achieved in our harmony with sisters and brothers with whom we practice. This harmony may be seen in outline in the Ten Grave Precepts of the Daughters and Sons of the Buddha.

The Precepts as Expressions of Love

At first it may seem that the Ten Precepts are negatively expressed commandments, like the Ten Commandments of Christianity and Judaism. However, they do not say, "Thou shalt not . . ." but rather "There is no . . . ." That is, in the mind there is no killing, no stealing, and so on. This does not mean merely that you should attain to that kind of relative condition where you are pure, but that in the mind, which is the universe, the Buddha-mind, there is no killing, no stealing, and so on, from the very beginning. Some commentaries by Dogen Zenji on the Ten Precepts carry the verb, "must not," but this can be understood to be for purposes of training. As a device, to reach realization that fundamentally there is no killing in the mind, you must not kill.

Even with their imperative implications, moral injunctions are expressions of love. It is an act of love, sometimes, to say, "Don't do that!" Either way, as a presentation of unity with all beings or as a corrective device, the Precepts are expressions of compassion, so we can say that the Ten Precepts are simply ten different ways of showing love.

The Ten Precepts formulate the realization of inherent good. This good is not the opposite of bad. It is self-nature, Buddha-nature. All beings by nature are Buddha—only their delusions and attachments prevent them from bearing witness to that fact. The Precepts are a guide from self-centered delusion and attachment to the Buddha's own full and complete realization of truth and compassion. They point the way to the fulfillment of your own Buddha nature.

The Application of the Precepts

Historically, the Ten Precepts, the Eightfold Path, and the other Buddhist injunctions were for the sake of disciples of Shakyamuni Buddha. They were to be applied individually and all beings might thus eventually be saved. In fact, all beings were saved with the enlightenment experience of each disciple. However, the Buddha did condemn the caste system and we find implicit in his teachings the futility of suppressing crime through punishment, the link between poverty and crime, and the importance of economic well-being for everyone. He did not live in a time like ours, when dangerous competition between nations threatens to blow up the world. He was not faced with the probability of biological holocaust. He did not encounter the righteous imperatives of a feminist movement. I wonder what he would say today.

In the West we have a clear sense of personal and group responsibility for the government and welfare of everyone, set forth by Locke, Rousseau, and others in the late eighteenth century and developed for the next two hundred years in democratic societies in Europe and the Americas. As Western Buddhists, we are building on one tradition of social responsibility that has been developing from Moses, Jesus, and Plato, and on another tradition that has been cultivated in monastic settings by yogis, Taoists, and Buddhists, as well as in the institutes of Confucianism, where highest probity was sought. With such a synthesis of traditions, Buddhism in the West is sure to apply the Precepts in a new way.

In the East too, we can see new beginnings of the Buddhist social contract. For example, the Sarvodaya Shramadana movement in Sri Lanka, starting from Buddhist ideals, seeks to build self-reliance in villages in matters of public health, public works, and arts and crafts. Monastic Buddhism, on the other hand, is clearly declining, and reformed Buddhism waters down the authentic truths of the founding teachers, permitting the poisons of acquisitive society to enter the bloodstream of the Buddha Dharma itself. It is important that we understand these changes.

The Ten Grave Precepts

1. No Killing. There is fundamentally no birth and no death as we die and are born. When we kill the spirit that may realize this fact, we are violating this precept. We kill that spirit in ourselves and in others when we brutalize human potential, animal potential, earth potential. We brutalize with a casual word or a look sometimes; it does not take a club or a bomb.

War and other acts of organized violence, including social repression, are massive violations of this precept. It is ironic that sometimes one can be considerate of the feelings of friends and neighbors while working at a job that directly contributes to widespread suffering.

At the other end of the scale, we find Jain monks who filter their water in an attempt not to harm microscopic creatures that inhabit it. Recent studies suggest that carrots and cabbages show responses to being cut or uprooted. What can we do? The answer is, I think, to eat and drink in the spirit of grateful sharing. I have heard that someone once asked Alan Watts why he was a vegetarian. He said, "Because cows scream louder than carrots." This reply may serve as a guideline. Some people will refuse to eat red meat. Some people will not drink milk. Some people will eat what is served to them, but will limit their own purchases of animal products. You must draw your own line, considering your health and the health of other beings.

2. No Stealing. There is no stealing and nothing to be stolen. To think possessively is a violation of this precept. The person who steals is misdirected in love and feels the need for something from others. Such a person must build justification for stealing, a structure of innocence, even though everyone is innocent from the beginning. Be true to that original innocence!

We live in an acquisitive society where it is impossible to survive without participating, indirectly at least, in thievery. This cannot be helped. We can only begin with ourselves to express our compassion for all creatures and things. Though even picking a flower is a kind of stealing, we pick it as we accept food for our table.

Like the Precept of No Killing, "No Stealing" has its application both in the immediate Buddha Sangha and outside in the workaday world. The Buddha's injunction in "The Eightfold Path" regarding "right vocation" urges a life of minimal exploitation. But our habits of consumption support massive and irredeemable exploitation of people, animals, trees, earth, water, and air. Great power is generated in support of this precept when people gather in a community and agree to conserve the energy of the universe and protect its beings and elements.

3. No Misuse of Sex. The mind—the universe-mind, which is the essential human mind—is pure, empty infinity. There is nothing to be called sexual exploitation there. We obscure this purity with clouds of coveting and scheming. Sex is sharing, but when it becomes using, it is perverted—a violation not only of this precept, but of the earlier two precepts as well, for it involves brutalizing and taking things of others. Like the thief, the person who indulges in casual sex may be seeking to draw something from outside. Another kind of casual sex rises from a lack of confidence in the self as the agent of the Dharma; it is a kind of false sharing, a prostitution.

People who have been conditioned by overliteral Catholic teaching or who have been followers of Yogananda or certain other Hindu teachers may come to Zen Buddhism with ideals of purity that interfere with the practice. The person for whom sexual purity is a psychological problem has little energy left over for zazen. Sex is neither pure nor impure. Our attitude about it can either be disruptive or conducive to deep practice. If two people are committed to one another, their sexual fulfillment in each other can be a positive support to their zazen.

4. No Lying. Under all circumstances, being true is first and foremost loyalty to the mind, to the emptiness, equality, and distinctiveness of all things. This mind, profound and subtle, appears in the phenomenal world with richness and variety. Efforts to deny or manipulate phenomena and obscure their essence violate this precept, for they set up a structure of justification, a cloud of words and thought, and the Buddha Dharma is nowhere to be seen.

But if a deranged person comes to the door in pursuit of someone within, I might lie and say the person being sought was not at home. To do so would be in support of this precept, for it would be in support of the intent of all the Precepts, which is to save all beings, to dissolve poisons, to realize the Dharma, and to attain the Buddha-Way.

5. No Dealing in Drugs. This Precept referred originally to alcohol, but of course it relates to anything that clouds our perceptions. Indulgence in TV or silly conversation would violate this precept. It is not possible for most people to do zazen after even a single glass of beer or a single puff from a marijuana cigarette, so we ban alcohol and dope at our Diamond Sangha training centers. The rules are, "No holding, no selling or giving away, and no using." The exception comes with occasional parties when a bottle of wine may be shared in toasting an honored guest. I have found by long observation that indulgence in marijuana as recreation on days off away from the training center can be detrimental to the practice, so I am now urging complete abstinence from this drug.

Smoking tobacco can be a problem at a training center. The smokers are distracted by their habit; the nonsmokers are distracted by the smell and by their isolation from those who smoke. Fundamentally, everything is empty and one, but we must also consider the setting necessary to realize that essential purity.

6. *No Speaking of Faults of Others.* Each individual is evolving and a fault can be the very place where the person can grow. This growth can be encouraged in many ways, but gossip leads to a stereotype and a folklore that divides the imperfect one from the rest of us. It blinds us to the development of maturity that our colleague may be cultivating through the very weakness that we condemn.

For example, if one of our friends becomes angry at the least provocation, that angry passion can with maturity be channeled into appropriate resistance to social injustice. But stereotyping such a person as "angry" may hinder our friend from maturing by prompting defensive justification. If the Tathagata is to be realized, we have to give him or her a chance.

7. *No Praising of Yourself While Abusing Others.* This is an extension of the preceding precept, pointing to a pernicious means of obscuring the reality that you and I are each completely individual and at the same time inseparably one in the organism of the universe. Where does the violation of this precept

come from? Its source again is a lack of confidence in the self as the agent of the Dharma. We seek to appear in a good light to defend ourselves at the expense of others.

This does not preclude correcting others. If someone is noisy during quiet time, we help to cultivate the practice with a reminder. The Precepts are not narrow injunctions; they always involve a well-developed sense of proportion.

The Sixth and Seventh Precepts are the easiest to violate. "All the world is queer save thee and me, and even thou are a little queer." Thus we separate from others, falling into the fundamental delusion of humanity.

8. No Sparing of Dharma Assets. Here the Dharma includes the teachings of the Buddha and all other things. The truth is aboundingly manifested about us. Obscuring that fact with self-centered talk and behavior is a violation of this precept.

To be free of self-centeredness is to be possessed of a broad and generous spirit that shares treasures from the bowl of the Buddha and the other things that come temporarily into our hands. Maezumi Roshi translates this precept, "Don't be stingy."[37]

Still, you count as one among all beings. I count as one also. I might help you to buy a typewriter, but you cannot have the one in my study. I need that for my work.

9. No Indulgence in Anger. There is actually no anger and no one at whom to get angry, but in the rather demanding circumstances of Zen training we find old traumas flaring up anew, so sometimes anger is our total environment. It cannot be helped. Anger is one of the emotions and emotion is the nature of vitality. If we recognize that our feelings rise from within and are not necessarily justified by what is happening outside, we can change through the acknowledgment, "This is my fault."

Occasionally, however, we raise the voice and assume a

stern countenance. In appropriate circumstances, where the practice of others may be enhanced, this is not a violation of the precept. However, self-indulgent anger, freely vented, separates, rather than brings people together.

Closely allied to anger is hatred, or holding a grudge, which is the perpetuation of an anger that somehow feeds the self-esteem, just as greed may feed ego-preoccupation, and clinging to error may protect a self-image. Hatred is a poison that permanently sets people apart, creating and justifying violations of all the Precepts, smothering any possibility of compassion.

10. No Slandering of the Three Treasures. The Buddha, Dharma, and Sangha are above slander, of course; the slander itself is the Three Treasures. But it takes an opened eye to see this. Wanton slander of realization, the way, and the fellowship may destroy the enthusiasm of earnest students and block their paths to realization.

Gossip can harm the very tissue of the Sangha. Inappropriate behavior as Buddhists can also be damaging. Every Zen Buddhist student is a leader of the Sangha, influencing all other students, but old-timers in particular have an important responsibility. Their action sets the tone at the training center and the Three Treasures are brightened or dimmed accordingly in the minds of all of us.

Confidentiality

In addition to the classic Precepts, I should like to add one more, the Precept of Silence about Personal Practice. This caution is emphasized at all training centers, yet it is often violated.

There is nothing more distracting to a Zen student than to hear, "Roshi said thus-and-so to me." Those words were directed to that student alone and may be inappropriate for another person. If they were words of approval, then there is an implied put-down of others. Be considerate of others—keep your practice personal.

Keeping silent about one's practice keeps the Sangha from becoming competitive and elitist. It is not necessary to speak of passing koans in order to establish yourself as a Zen student. Hold all such matters private between yourself and your teacher.

Of course the spirit of "hush-hush" can be overdone and it can contribute to a lot of distracting speculation. The fact that someone is doing well in the practice is evident to everyone. There is no need to deny it. Cultivate a sense of proportion.

Zen and Ethics

I have heard some people say that since Zen says we must be grounded in the place where there is no right and wrong, it follows that Zen has no ethical application. But if there were no application of our experience of the unity and the individuality of all beings, then Zen would be only a stale exercise in seclusion, the way of death. Yamada Roshi says, "The purpose of Zen is the perfection of character." It is a way to realize self-nature—and its application lies in the practice of harmony in the everyday world. At the training center, all conditions of the world are present. If you can cope there socially, you are doing very well.

I am reminded of the story about "Bird's Nest Roshi." He was a teacher who lived in the T'ang period and did zazen in a tree. The governor of his province, Po Chü-i, heard about Bird's Nest Roshi and went to see him. This Po Chu-i was no ordinary politician. He was one of China's greatest poets, well known for his expression of Zen Buddhism.

Po Chu-i found Bird's Nest Roshi sitting in his tree, doing zazen. He called to him, saying, "Oh, Bird's Nest, you look very insecure to me up there."

Bird's Nest Roshi looked down at Po Chu-i and replied, "Oh Governor, you look very insecure to me down there." All things are under the law of change and political position is the most ephemeral of all. Po Chu-i knew very well what Bird's Nest Roshi was talking about. So he took a different tack.

"Tell me," he said, "What is it that all the Buddhas taught?" Bird's Nest Roshi replied by quoting from the *Dhammapada*:

> Always do good;
> never do evil;
> keep your mind pure—
> thus all the Buddhas taught.

So Po Chu-i said, "Always do good; never do evil; keep your mind pure—I knew that when I was three years old."

"Yes," said Bird's Nest Roshi, "A three-year-old child may know it, but even an eighty-year-old man cannot put it into practice."[38]

Perfection of character comes with the realization of a pure mind, but as Hui-neng said, with an ordinary thought you are (again) an ordinary person.[39] Practice in daily life is the same as practice on your cushions: check your ordinary thoughts of greed, hatred, and ignorance and return to your original, pure mind. Like Zen study generally, character change is a lifetime work. And to return to Yamada Roshi's words, Zen study is character change.

CHAPTER EIGHT

Establishing
the Practice

Zen practice is a matter of change from ignorance of Buddha-nature to its realization. This involves letting go of the
self and uniting with the object of attention. In the history of
Zen Buddhism, only the founder, Shakyamuni Buddha himself, came to full maturity without at least a touch from a
teacher. The Sixth Great Ancestor, Hui-neng, and a few other
geniuses appeared in a setting or culture of illuminative vigor
and required only confirmation of their own realization by a
true teacher. The rest of us need guidance. I find that the
person who says that no teacher is necessary usually is not ready
to begin zazen.

The Role of the Rōshi

It is important from the beginning to understand the function
of the roshi. To begin with, the title, "Roshi," simply means
"old teacher." It is as much an expression of endearment as it is
an official title. It does not mean *guru,* and the distinction is
important.

The roshi is a guide through unknown lands. Just as a guide
through a tropical jungle must be firm in requiring certain
conduct, so the roshi will urge certain ways to practice. Since
the object of zazen is the falling away of the ordinary self in the
act of uniting with breath counting or the koan, the roshi
stands to one side and encourages the student to experience

this falling away. When the self does fall away completely, it can be a wonderful experience. The roshi then encourages the student to understand that experience and to learn how to present it in all circumstances.

The guru, too, encourages falling away, but in the act of identifying with the guru. The guru is omnipotent, and though he or she may try to encourage the student to find independence, the Dharma will have a specific name and face and the student cannot truly be free.

I may not be making an accurate presentation of guru-student relationships that would apply in all cases, but I want to show that the roshi wishes each person to develop to the highest potential. The roshi is not interested in being deified and will refuse to be placed in such a position.

Faith in the Rōshi

Just as one must have faith in one's guide in order to traverse an unknown forest, so faith in the roshi is essential. This is not a matter of personal aggrandizement for the roshi, but a matter of utmost importance for the student. Without that faith, zazen becomes only a sterile practice in concentration, with no movement toward realization and beyond. The student cannot trust himself or herself truly to let go.

It is like the new diver on the high board. The coach says, "Go ahead, dive off." If the athlete trusts the coach, then letting go, at least in that dimension, is possible. If not, then retreat is the only option. The roshi will have foibles, like any other human being. But faith in the roshi is not a matter of expecting perfection.

Not interested in proselytizing, the roshi is glad if a student finds a true home with another Zen teacher. Once you are established, however, there is a certain etiquette involved in changing teachers. See your roshi about this and request a referral. This is a matter-of-fact arrangement made for the sake of the student. There need be no apologies and there will be no recriminations. From earliest times, students have made such arrangements, sometimes at the suggestion of their original teachers.

This is quite different from "sesshin-hopping." Lightly moving from teacher to teacher is a waste of energy all around, for the student cannot settle down. And that's what zazen is, after all: settling down.

The relationship between roshi and student is a matter of mutual investment. If you foresee changes in your life that will affect your practice, such as moving away from the Sangha, be sure to let your teacher know in advance.

How to Connect

When I was a classroom teacher I always felt there was more hope for the student who threw a piece of chalk at me when my back was turned than for the one who put his head down on his desk. That piece of chalk gave me a chance to do something, to say something. But what can one do if there is no response? In meeting with the roshi, it is important that you speak up and show something. Don't try to conjure up a question, however. If you have nothing to say, just come and say, "I have nothing to say." That is a complete presentation.

The heart of Zen Buddhism, indeed the heart of other religions also, lies in dialogue. Such dialogue is designed for the purpose of awakening the student. It is not designed to support the self-esteem of either party.

> A monk said to Yüeh-shan Wei-yen, "I have a problem. Will you solve it for me?"
>
> Yueh-shan said, "I will solve it for you tonight."
>
> That evening, Yueh-shan ascended to the high seat and said, "Will the monk who has a problem step forward."

The monk stepped forward. Yueh-shan descended from his seat, grasped the monk by the lapels of his robe, shook him, and called out, "Oh, monks, this fellow has a problem!" Then he pushed him away and walked out.[40]

Don't misunderstand this story. The roshi was responding directly and mercifully to the monk's request. The roshi's consciousness is the content of the story, and that is the consciousness you must show to your own roshi when you work on it as a koan. But Yueh-shan was also saying something about problems in general. If there is no problem, there is no anxiety; if there is no anxiety, where will you find the energy for your practice?

A practical problem may arise, such as, "My mother is sick—should I go home to see her or remain here at the training center?" Such a matter can be talked over with the roshi at quite a different level. The roshi would then be an advisor, a different role. A trusted senior member of the Sangha could also serve in such a role.

Shōken and Dokusan

After you have completed the orientation course and after you have heard the roshi give a *teishō* (Dharma talk) and, perhaps, after you have met him or her informally, you have experienced enough to know whether you wish to make this roshi your Zen teacher. If you decide affirmatively, arrangements are made for you to have *shōken,* your first formal interview. This differs widely from center to center.

In the Diamond Sangha tradition, three deep bows are made in the course of the usual *dokusan* (interview). However, at shoken, you make nine deep bows and offer incense money as a token of your investment in the roshi as your teacher.

The roshi will ask you why you wish to do zazen. This is an

important question and you should be prepared in advance to answer it. However, if you have no answer, that is all right. Just say so; that is an answer.

The point is that the roshi wants to relate his way of teaching to your needs. He or she will ask you your age, marital status, occupation, and so on, by way of getting acquainted. But the main question is, "What brings you here?"

Once, at the Maui Zendo, some people had a flat tire on the road in front of the temple. They came in to use the telephone and stayed six months. There is significance in each human encounter so you need not try to conjure up a deep reason for coming.

The roshi wants to provide teaching that is appropriate for you. It is no good feeding curry to someone with ulcers. Find your own way to show how you stand. After you have made your presentation, the roshi will suggest a practice for you, one of the styles of zazen you have already tried, or the koan "Mu." There will be time for questions at the end of the interview, but you may interrupt the conversation with questions at any point. Questions will come to your mind later, and you may return to dokusan with them.

Yasutani Roshi used to say that questions about the best book to read for the study of Zen, or questions about Buddhist philosophy, might not be appropriate to raise in the dokusan room. He would continue, "If you want to know why your teeth hurt or your belly growls when you do zazen, I will be happy to discuss such matters with you." My own way is to permit any question and to make an appointment to discuss time-consuming subjects at a more convenient hour. At dokusan, we have only a few minutes of interaction—many people come, one after another, in a relatively short period of time.

There are simple procedures to follow in the dokusan room

that you will rehearse in advance with a senior member of the Sangha. The gist of them is openness and respect. You should be ready to change. The bows, in which you throw everything away, are your acts of readiness.

In Conclusion

In our Diamond Sangha centers, you may choose to come to meetings without ever having shoken or dokusan. The only restriction is that you may not attend sesshin unless you have started to work with the roshi. Other Zen centers may be more strict in such matters.

I should like now to have you return to breath counting in your zazen. You may choose to count your exhalations only or to count both inhalations and exhalations.

You are setting out on a great adventure, your own departure into the forest of Zen practice. Like our founder, Shakyamuni Buddha, you will experience both discouragement and insight. And like Shakyamuni and his successors, you can one day hope to see into your own essential nature and the essential nature of all beings and things.

The first step is the same in content as the last. Don't keep progress and development at the forefront of your mind. Each breath, each point is the sequence of your counting—that is immensity itself.

CHAPTER NINE

The Koan Mu

You have been introduced to the rationale and method of Zen practice. Now I offer the koan "Mu," which students specifically interested in realization may take up under the guidance of a roshi after they are grounded in breath counting. It comes from the *Wu Mên Kuan,* a collection of classical Zen cases with commentaries put together by Wu-men Hui-k'ai in the early twelfth century.

THE CASE
A monk asked Chao-chou, "Has the dog Buddha-nature or not?"

Chao-chou said, "Mu."

WU-MEN'S COMMENT
For the practice of Zen, it is imperative that you pass through the barrier set up by the ancestral teachers. For subtle realization, it is of the utmost importance that you cut off the mind road. If you do not pass the barrier of the ancestors; if you do not cut off the mind road—then you are a ghost clinging to bushes and grasses.

What is the barrier of the ancestral teachers? It is just this one word, Mu, the one barrier of our faith. We call it the "Gateless Barrier of the Zen Sect." When you pass through this barrier, you will not only interview Chao-chou intimately, you will walk hand in hand with all the ancestral teachers in the successive generations of our lineage, the hair of your eyebrows entangled with theirs, seeing with the same eyes, hearing with the same ears. Won't that be joyous? Is there anyone who would not want to pass this barrier?

So then, make your whole body a mass of doubt, and with your 360 bones and joints and your 84,000 hair follicles, concentrate on this one word Mu. Day and night, keep digging into it. Don't consider it to be nothingness. Don't think in terms of "has" or "has not." It is like swallowing a red-hot iron ball. You try to vomit it out, but you cannot. Gradually you purify yourself, eliminating mistaken knowledge and attitudes you have held from the past. Inside and outside become one, and you are like a dumb person who has had a dream. You know it for yourself alone.

Suddenly Mu breaks open. The heavens are astonished; the earth is shaken. It is as though you snatch away the great sword of General Kuan. When you meet the Buddha, you kill the Buddha. When you meet Bodhidharma, you kill Bodhidharma. At the very cliff-edge of birth and death, you find the Great Freedom. In the six worlds and in the four modes of birth, you can enjoy a samadhi of frolic and play.

So, how should you work with it? Exhaust all your life-energy on this one word Mu. If you do not falter, then it's done! A single spark lights your Dharma candle.

WU-MEN'S VERSE

> Dog! Buddha nature!
> The perfect presentation of the whole.
> With a bit of "has" or "has not,"
> body is lost; Life is lost. [41]

Chao-chou Ts'ung-shen

Chao-chou (Japanese: Jōshū) was a remarkable teacher in a remarkable era. He lived in the T'ang period, the golden age of Zen for almost 120 years (778 to 897). Zen teachers are noted for their longevity, and many in the past lived into their eighties and nineties at a time when the human life span was considered to be fifty years. You may say that longevity is a physical phenomenon, a combination of good genes, good diet, and so on. I won't argue the point. Suspend your judgement and look at his life story.

Chao-chou was ordained as a young boy and came to study with Nan-ch'uan P'u-yuan when he was eighteen. At the time, Nan-ch'uan was not feeling well, so their first interview was held in his bedroom, with Nan-ch'uan in bed.

> Nan-ch'uan asked him, "Where have you been recently?"
> Chao-chou said, "At Shui-hsiang [literally, *Auspicious Image*]."
> Nan-ch'uan asked, "Did you see the Auspicious Image?"
> Chao-chou said, "I did not see the Image, but I have seen a reclining Tathagata."[42]

The dialogue continued, but Nan-ch'uan had already recognized the young man's promise. Chao-chou remained with Nan-ch'uan until the teacher died, forty years later. After the requisite two years of mourning, Chao-chou set out on pilgrimage to visit the outstanding teachers of his time to deepen and clarify his insight in Dharma dialogues.

When he started out on his pilgrimage, Chao-chou announced, "If I meet a seven-year-old child who can teach me, I will stay there and be that child's student. If I meet a 100-year-old man who seeks my guidance, I will be his teacher." Against the background of Confucian veneration of elders and patronage of children, you can appreciate Chao-chou's modesty and resolution to become worthy as a disciple of the Buddha.

Finally, at the age of eighty, he settled down, accepted students, and taught another forty years. Thus, even at the beginning of his teaching career, Chao-chou was very old and lacked strength to shout or beat his students. His way is called the "Zen of the Lips." It is said that a light seemed to play about his mouth when he spoke. Dogen Zenji, who was rigorous in his criticism of his predecessors, had only the highest praise for Chao-chou and referred to him as "Chao-chou, the old Buddha."

The Dialogue

We can be sure that the monk who asked about the Buddha nature of the dog knew very well that all beings by nature are Buddha. This is set forth clearly in sutras, some of which the monk probably chanted every day. But he had not yet experienced that fact. He was thinking that, really, Buddha nature is something to be attained. Perhaps he had mused, "Shakyamuni Buddha sat under the Bodhi tree six long years before he attained to Buddha-nature. My teacher, Chao-chou, studied with his teacher for forty years and then wandered for another twenty years before he was confident of his Buddha-nature. As for me, I don't think I have Buddha-nature at this time." By way of presenting his doubt in the most concrete way possible, he asked Chao-chou, "Has the dog Buddha nature?" Do you mean to tell me that miserable dog is a Buddha from the beginning?

For "Buddha-nature," read "essential nature, true nature, self-nature." Really the monk is asking, "What is Buddha-nature?" A most fundamental question.

Chao-chou said, "Mu."[43] Mu means, "No," or, "Does not have," but Chao-chou was not responding at the level of ordinary meaning. He was showing Buddha-nature with his brief response, and he was also showing how to practice. "Muuuuuuuu"—softly in his presentation, silently on your cushions—breathe Mu in and out. Or just exhale Mu, and keep your mind steady and quiet on your inhalations.

When you first sit down, count your breaths from "one" to "ten" in your usual way. Do this for one or more sequences until your mind is reasonably quiet, then take up Mu. Remember: it is not that you are focusing on Mu. That would be two things. Let Mu breathe Mu. You must become completely intimate with Mu.

The Comment

Although Mu was certainly a popular koan before the *Wu Men Kuan* was published (Wu-men himself worked on it for six years), it is "Wu-men's Comment" that established the word as the important first barrier for all students interested in realization. Yamada Roshi points out that the Comment is unique among all Zen writings, in that it sets forth a condensed explanation of how to do zazen that is not found elsewhere. Thus it is precious and deserves our careful study.

For the practice of Zen, it is imperative that you pass through the barrier set up by the ancestral teachers. This sentence sums up the spirit of what may be called "Koan Zen," that is, the Zen that practices realization through focus on a single word or phrase or action set forth by an old teacher. You may attain deep and quiet samadhi, you may master all the abstruse formulations of Buddhist philosophy, you may have a broad and generous spirit, but you still must see the point of Mu, the point of Chu-chih's upraised finger, the point of Yueh-shan's walking out.

For subtle realization, it is of the utmost importance that you cut off the mind road. The word I translate here as "subtle" may also be rendered "wonderful." For such an experience of essential nature, you must cut your train of thought.

> A monk asked Chao-chou, "How should I use the twenty-four hours?"
> Chao-chou said, "You are used by the twenty-four hours. I use the twenty-four hours."[44]

You are used by the twenty-four hours because you are used by your thoughts. A train of thought passes through your head twenty-four hours a day, manipulating you. Turn this condition around and cultivate a quiet mind that may evoke thoughts appropriate to circumstances.

The process of this turnabout is zazen, in which you become intimate with Mu and all random thoughts die down of themselves. This is not the act of rooting out the source of thoughts. It is the cultivation of peace that passes all understanding, which gives rise to a true sense of proportion.

A longtime Zen friend wrote me of her experience of cutting off the mind road:

> Things are going very smoothly for me now. For one thing, I'm so busy that I can't think about anything more than what to have for lunch tomorrow, and how to get rid of all those leftovers, but also, for the first time really, I can actually feel movement in my practice. I read in the last Don Juan book about how the key to everything is "stopping the internal dialogue," and somehow it struck me and I started doing it. Immediately I had this vivid experience of being the sole creator of all my thoughts and feelings and therefore in total control. All I have to do any time is to shut off the internal dialogue and the voices don't exist any more. It's not that they're still there and I'm "just not going to think about it"—they're really not there if *I'm* not there. Suddenly all the situations I never thought I could handle are not even Situations any more, in that heavy sense, though actually nothing has changed.

After many years of zazen, my friend learned to use the twenty-four hours. It does not always take so long.

If you do not pass the barrier of the ancestors, if you do not cut off the mind road, then you are a ghost clinging to bushes and grasses. When you are used by your thoughts, your feet are not planted firmly on the ground, in fact you have no feet at all. Your are only the shadow of a human being, blown about by circumstances, clinging to concepts of birth and death, cause and effect, priestly and secular, inside and outside. You there, with the wind whistling through your nightie, what is your original self?

What is the barrier of the ancestral teachers? Don't presume that "barrier" means "barricade." See your dictionary. The meaning of "barrier" here is "checkpoint," as at a frontier. The way is completely open. "Show me how you stand with yourself. Show me how you stand with the universe. Okay, you may go along." It is that kind of barrier.

You may say that everything is such a barrier. When your spouse yells at you, that is a barrier. When your car breaks down on the freeway, that is a barrier. So some Zen students say everything is a koan. That is true, but we are faced with so many everyday-life koans that we have no way to deal with them. It is of the utmost importance that we cut off this train of problems on our cushions, and sink into Mu. Then we may find that our workaday koans are really transparent and insubstantial.

It is just this one word Mu, the one barrier of our faith. This is a "single word of a single syllable," which the anonymous author of *The Cloud of Unknowing* suggests you take up in your meditation. He proposed "God," or "love," or "sin." But such words are loaded with meaning, and meaning may tend to keep you conjecturing. As Yamada Roshi says, "Mu has no meaning whatsoever." Thus it is a barrier peculiar to the Zen path.

Make no mistake, Mu is meaning*ful*. It can be identified, pointed to, personified. It is like swimming. You can say what swimming is. You can mime swimming. But does it have a meaning? Once I took a course in swimming at the University of Hawaii. Every week, we spent three hours in the pool and one hour in class. In the pool we swam, and that was swimming. In the class we studied musculature and diagrams of fishes. I felt it had nothing to do with swimming. In the same way, this book has nothing to do with Zen.

We call it the "Gateless Barrier of the Zen Sect." "Gateless Barrier" is also the translation of the title of the book, the *Wu Men Kuan,* and Wu-men's name means "gateless." Wu-men said that he did not arrange his cases in the *Wu Men Kuan* in any particular order, but he did place "Chou-chou's Dog" first, and here he declares that Mu is the one barrier of the Zen way. Countless Zen students have proved this in their own practice.

When I started out in my own practice, I thought that "gateless" meant impenetrable. What a great mistake! The Chinese thrush sings loudly and clearly in the early morning. That's it! A ripe breadfruit lands "thump!" on our roof in the middle of the night. That's it!

When you pass through this barrier, you will not only interview Chao-chou intimately, you will walk hand in hand with all the ancestral teachers in the successive generations of our lineage, the hair of your eyebrows entangled with theirs, seeing with the same eyes, hearing with the same ears. You will not only have intimate dokusan with Chao-chou, you will tangle eyebrows with all the old worthies. This does not mean that you will be so close to them that your eyebrows will brush against theirs. It means that your eyebrows and their eyebrows will be one and the same.

Not only will you find intimacy with the ancestral teachers. You will find that mountains, rivers, and the great earth itself are not separate from your act of rolling out of bed. In Japanese dokusan rooms, students are presented with the koan, "Let Mt. Fuji dance!" What happens to the surrounding villages at such a time?

So then, make your whole body a mass of doubt, and with your 360 bones and joints and your 84,000 hair follicles, concentrate on this one word Mu. In Zen literature you will find references to the three requirements of Zen practice, great doubt, great faith, and great zeal.[45] All right, I agree these are important, but they are generally interpreted only on the level of step-by-step training. Many people have problems with them, thinking, "Is my doubt, my spirit of inquiry, strong enough? Do I have enough faith? Am I earnest enough?" Remember Yasutani Roshi's words, "Five percent sincerity is enough." The fact that you are earnest enough to come to the center to sit with us is sufficient. You can build your sincerity from here on.

Yamada Roshi says "great doubt" means "becoming one with Mu." I would say that "great faith" is the act of bowing at the door of the dojo. "Great zeal" is the act of rocking back and forth in decreasing arcs before you take up breath counting. Don't overdramatize your practice or set up unreasonable targets.

Nonetheless, it is imperative that you pass through the barrier. Use all your energy in this task. This does not mean that you should strain. Just don't use energy on anything except Mu.

Day and night, keep digging into it. This is sesshin advice. You get up at 4:00 AM and go to bed at 9:00 PM, keeping Mu at the forefront of your mind in zazen, in kinhin, during meals, and at rest time. However, even at sesshin, you may be called upon to do a task that requires all your attention. If you focus on Mu as you chop carrots, you may cut yourself. At such a time, focus only on the chopping, that is your practice.

In the same way, in your workaday life you will have mini-sesshins in the early morning and in the evening, but during the rest of your time you are busy with your job and your family. One of the ways of checking students working on Mu teaches us how to practice in such times, "Explain Mu so that a baby can understand." Crooning "Muuuu" is not the correct response.

When your are driving a car, just drive, keeping yourself alert to all exigencies. When you answer the telephone, devote yourself to the caller. Likewise, move from circumstance to circumstance with this same quality of attention. Practice awareness.

However, there may be times when you have a short break.

You are waiting for a bus, walking down the hall, waiting for the next client. At such times you can breathe Mu quietly, without calling attention to yourself. Even in the midst of a task, you will have space for what Katsuki Sekida used to call "one-breath Mu." A single sigh, "Muuuuuuu," and you return to your work refreshed and aware.

Don't consider it to be nothingness. Don't think in terms of "has" or "has not." You understand this by now, but the implication of these cautions goes beyond the koan. There are some people who fall into the pit of emptiness and keep repeating, "It doesn't matter," or "It's all one." During the drug revolution of the late 1960s and early 1970s, I met many young men and women who were caught in this trap. Sometimes a religious experience will lead you into such a state. A "sick soul" condition, it can be very persuasive. I agree that everything is empty, but at the same time it is also full. It is sometimes high and sometimes low, sometimes strong and sometimes weak, sometimes light and sometimes dark. Don't let yourself get stuck in simplistic views.

Zen teachers like to tell the story of Yajñadatta, who always admired his face in a mirror. One day, he looked into the mirror and couldn't see himself. He thought he had lost his head and went rushing around, crying, "I haven't any head! I haven't any head!" His friends caught him and held him, seeking to persuade him that he did indeed have a head. Finally, one of them hit him over the head. With the pain he suddenly realized that his head was firmly in place. Rushing around again, he cried, "I have a head after all!"[46] The usual moral of this story is that you have essential nature from the very beginning, but you don't know it, and you need to settle down, listen to teisho, and get a jolt from the roshi to realize what has always been true. But for our purposes here, to say "I have no essential nature" or "I have essential nature after all" are both incorrect.

It is like a red-hot iron ball. You try to vomit it out, but you cannot. This is Wu-men's description of a certain point in the ripening process of koan study. Mu sits there in your gut. You no longer breathe Mu in and out. Mu breathes Mu in and out. You know you can't get rid of Mu at that point and you don't want to anyway. You just sit Mu, stand Mu, walk Mu. You feel that Mu has its own imperative. What is it? Mu.

Gradually, you purify yourself, eliminating mistaken knowledge and attitudes you have held from the past. What are the mistaken knowledge and attitudes you have held from the past? Dogen Zenji said, "That the self advances and confirms the ten thousand things is called delusion."[47] We suppose that people, animals, and things fall into categories and concepts, forgetting that we ourselves create those categories and concepts. They really do not exist except in the human cortex. When we act as though the neighboring gang, or the neighboring country, is dangerous, it becomes dangerous. When men project roles upon women, then only the most resolute escape. Thus we divide up the universe and limit its potential.

With zazen, focusing only on Mu, empty oneness that underlies and infuses all things is taken to heart. When you hear "Russian," you don't necessarily see red. When someone says, "Ladies first," you can enjoy a good laugh. Your fixations are starting to melt.

Inside and outside become one. One of my students reported to me that he experienced himself as a wicker ball while sitting on his cushions. This may seem bizarre, but it was a genuine makyo, a deep dream of himself as a flimsy shell of basket weave, with emptiness inside and out. You may or may not have such a specific experience, but your sense of empty oneness will be clear.

You are like a dumb person who has had a dream. You know it for yourself alone. Mr. Sekida used to tell us about the time he and a friend were sitting on the verandah of the monastery, just at sunrise. It was the last day of a particularly deep and quiet sesshin. Of course, one does not speak during sesshin, but somehow the friend spoke anyway. "Oh," he said in a preoccupied way, "the sun has come up." This dreamy, forgetful condition may be another step on the path. Sometimes in dokusan, I will say to a student, "Show me Mu." The student may respond, "Muuuuuuuu," completely absorbed. A very promising condition.

Suddenly Mu breaks open. The heavens are astonished and the earth is shaken. Whammo! The breadfruit hits the tin roof! That's it! You see the point at last. A great surprise! The universe says, "Howdy!"

Some people think koan study is a matter of reaching an opinion about Mu and the succeeding cases of the practice. That is a little like saying you reach your own opinion about the content of a joke. Koans and jokes are not the same, but they share one characteristic. Each of them has a point. The point of Mu is the same for you and me and Yamada Roshi and his Japanese disciples and for all Zen students everywhere. *Precisely* the same. We are all members of the same nose-hole society. Essential nature is not a matter of opinion.

Pursuing our dubious joke analogy a little further, we see that some laughs are a guffaw, some are only a chuckle. Some realization experiences are deep, some are only a touch. Yasutani Roshi used to say that *kenshō,* the experience of seeing into true nature, is like rubbing a clear place on a piece of frosted glass. You peep through and that is essential nature all right. But you still must clean up all the impurities in the glass, and finally you push out the glass completely.

With that initial peep, you have a lifetime of work ahead of you. In terms of study in the Sanbo Kyodan tradition, more than 500 koans remain for you to make your own. Indeed, at a ceremony for someone who had completed his koan study,

Yasutani Roshi remarked, "His practice has just started."

When he was eighty-six, Yamamoto Gempō Roshi took up again the practice of reading the *Diamond Sutra* aloud. On one occasion, he pointed to a passage and remarked to his attendant, "Now at last I understand that point." It is popularly said by Zen people, "Shakyamuni Buddha is still practicing, and he is only halfway there."

Resolving the koan Mu is an important milestone. It may be said that there are two kinds of koans, the first one and all the others. Once past the first milestone, the others are a little easier, since you know their basic spirit. It is not unusual to find true resonance with a so-called advanced koan in just a single dokusan, though often more time is necessary, and sometimes one gets stuck and must stay there for a while.

It is as though you snatch away the great sword of General Kuan. Wu-men is having his little joke here. General Kuan is a famous military figure in Chinese history, but his name is written with the same ideograph as *kuan,* meaning "barrier." You have snatched away the barrier itself. You are king or queen of the mountain now. You are sitting alone at Ta Hsiung Peak. It is said that when he was born, the baby Buddha raised one hand pointing above, lowered the other pointing below, and announced, "Above the heavens, below the heavens, only I, alone and sacred." This is the Arhat experience, solitary and sustained in the vast universe.

When you meet the Buddha, you kill the Buddha. When you meet Bodhidharma, you kill Bodhidharma. This is a widely misunderstood passage. In context, it has two correct interpretations. From a karmic view, it means that you wipe away the thought of the Buddha or an ancestral teacher. What are you doing here, old Bodhidharma? Get away!

From the essential view, there are no Buddhas or ancestral teachers at all:

The attendant K'uo asked Te-shan Hsüan-chien, "Where have all the Buddhas and ancestral teachers gone?"

Te-shan asked, "What did you say?"

K'uo said, "I commanded an exceedingly fine racehorse to spring forth, but only a lame tortise appeared."

Te-shan said nothing.[48]

What is the difference in insight between Te-shan and his attendant? I think the attendant knew very well about karmic and essential views, but Te-shan had forgotten them completely.

At the very cliff-edge of birth and death, you find the Great Freedom. Once a student came to me and said he was depressed because he had realized that there is nothing to depend upon. I laughed, and he asked why I was laughing. I said, "Why do you think the old Zen worthies were always clowning around?" He laughed. The biggest joke in the universe is that there is nothing to depend upon. When you see that joke, then you are free to get up when the alarm clock goes off.

In the six worlds and in the four modes of birth, you enjoy a samadhi of frolic and play. The six worlds of conventional Buddhism are the realms of hell, hungry ghosts, animals, demons, human beings, and heaven. The four modes of birth in old Buddhist physiology were the womb-born, the egg-born, the moisture-born, and the metamorphosis-born. Wherever! Whenever! Hakuin Zenji said, "Singing and dancing are the voice of the Dharma."[49] Wu-men turns this around and says, "The voice of the Dharma is singing and dancing." Hooray for composting and cooking!

So, how should you work with it? Exhaust all your life-energy on this one word Mu. You must take this advice literally. One of my Zen friends in Japan uses the expression, "One hundred percent combustion." Burn all your fuel in this fire of Mu. Straining, however, is a different matter. When you strain, you become exhausted. Still, that is the way some people must go at first, strain, blow-out, strain, blow-out. Get past that stage if you can and reach a constant force of concentration and identification. Only Mu. Only Mu. There is only Mu inside, only Mu outside, only Mu in the whole universe.

If you do not falter, then it's done. Some people read a reversed message here, "If it isn't done, then I must be faltering." That is not correct. You are cultivating your dojo, your body and mind as the holy place of enlightenment. Once, when I was discouraged about my practice, Nakagawa Roshi quoted Chao-chou to me: "If you follow my instructions carefully, and do not realize anything in twenty years, then you may dig up my skull and use it as a nightsoil dipper." Nightsoil is human excrement that is cured as fertilizer. We'll let your bones rest in peace, old Chao-chou.

A single spark lights your Dharma candle. What is that single spark? The gecko, "Chi! Chi! Chi! Chichichichi!" The thud of the breadfruit. A whiff of incense. Are you ready? "The readiness is all."

The Verse

> Dog! Buddha nature!
> The perfect presentation of the whole!

When you become truly intimate with Mu, then you can take up these lines with your roshi. What is that perfect presentation? Show me! The whole universe must come forth!

> With a bit of "has" or "has not,"
> Body is lost; life is lost.

Turn this verse around. When body and life are lost, there is not a bit of "has" or "has not." When you truly experience the Great Death, you will find the Great Life is not limited by such dichotomies as "has" and "has not," cause and effect, even death and life.

Avalokiteshvara Bodhisattva, practicing deep prajna
    paramita,
clearly saw that all five skandas are empty, transforming all
    suffering and distress.
Shariputra, form is no other than emptiness, emptiness no
    other than form;
form is exactly emptiness, emptiness exactly form;
sensation, thought, impulse, consciousness are also like this.
Shariputra, all things are marked by emptiness—not born,
    not destroyed;
not stained, not pure; without gain, without loss.
Therefore, in emptiness there is no form, no sensation,
    thought, impulse, consciousness;
no eye, ear, nose, tongue, body, mind;
no color, sound, smell, taste, touch, object of thought;
no realm of sight to no realm of thought;
no ignorance and also no ending of ignorance
to no old age and death and also no ending of old age and death;
no suffering, also no source of suffering, no annihilation, no
    path;
no wisdom, also no attainment. Having nothing to attain,
Bodhisattvas live prajna paramita
with no hindrance in the mind. No hindrance, thus no fear.
Far beyond delusive thinking, they attain complete Nirvana.

110

All Buddhas past, present, and future live prajna paramita
and thus attain anuttara samyak sambodhi.
Therefore, know that prajna paramita is
the great mantra, the wisdom mantra,
the unsurpassed mantra, the supreme mantra,
which completely removes all suffering.
This is truth, not deception.
Therefore, set forth the prajna paramita mantra,
set forth this mantra and say:
"Gate, gate, pāragate, pārasaṃgate, bodhi svāhā!"

All beings by nature are Buddha,
as ice by nature is water.
Apart from water there is no ice;
apart from beings, no Buddha.

How sad that people ignore the near
and search for truth afar:
like someone in the midst of water
crying out in thirst;
like a child of a wealthy home
wandering among the poor.

Lost on dark paths of ignorance,
we wander through the Six Worlds;
from dark path to dark path—
when shall we be freed from birth and death?

Oh, the zazen of the Mahayana!
To this the highest praise!
Devotion, repentance, training,
the many paramitas—
all have their source in zazen.

Those who try zazen even once
wipe away beginningless crimes.

112

Where are all the dark paths then?
The Pure Land itself is near.

Those who hear this truth even once
and listen with a grateful heart,
treasuring it, revering it,
gain blessings without end.

Much more, those who turn about
and bear witness to self-nature,
self-nature that is no-nature,
go far beyond mere doctrine.

Here effect and cause are the same;
the Way is neither two nor three.
With form that is no-form,
going and coming, we are never astray;
with thought that is no-thought,
even singing and dancing are the voice of the Law.

How boundless and free is the sky of Samadhi!
How bright the full moon of wisdom!
Truly, is anything missing now?
Nirvana is right here, before our eyes;
this very place is the Lotus Land;
this very body, the Buddha.

APPENDIX:

Willy-Nilly Zen*

It began when an acquaintance remarked that my writings reminded him of Oriental poetry. I borrowed translations of Japanese and Chinese literature from the library, and met Basho and Po Chu-i.

Then World War II came along and I found myself caught as a civilian on the island of Guam, taken to Japan, and interned in Kobe. The guards of our camp discovered my interest in haiku, and when R. H. Blyth's *Zen in English Literature* was published late in 1942, one of them loaned me a copy.

I was fascinated by the point of view expressed in this book. I read it over and over, perhaps ten times, and underwent many strange experiences that enabled me to read Shakespeare, Basho, and other profound writers as though for the first time. The world seemed transparent, and I was absurdly happy despite our miserable circumstances.

Dr. Blyth was also interned in Kobe, and when all the camps in the city were combined in May, 1944, we were confined together with 175 other enemy nationals above the city. For the next fourteen months, until the war was over, I learned much about Zen from this creative teacher and I deter-

*I prepared this record at Yamada Roshi's request in November, 1971. It is presented here with very little editing, with footnotes and an afterword added to explain a bit and bring things up to date. Terms not defined earlier may be found in the Glossary.

115

mined that I would do zazen under the guidance of a roshi when I could find the opportunity.

After being returned to the United States, I reentered the University of Hawaii and was graduated in 1947 with a degree in English literature. I got married that year and with my wife traveled to Berkeley for study in Japanese literature and language.

One of my friends was interested in Krishnamurti, an Indian teacher whose point of view can be compared to Zen. He persuaded me to go with him during the Christmas vacation of 1947 to Southern California to try to find this teacher. We visited Ojai, a town north of Los Angeles where Krishnamurti lived when he was in the United States, but Krishnamurti was then in India.

We traveled further south and I stopped in at the Oriental bookshop of P. D. and Ione Perkins in South Pasadena. There I met Richard A. Gard, now a well-known scholar of Buddhism. He was then head clerk of the shop and was earning his doctorate from Claremont College. We had known each other as fellow students at the University of Hawaii before the war.

I was interested to see the large collection of Zen books, mostly by Dr. D. T. Suzuki, that the bookshop had for sale and I asked Mr. Gard if he knew of any Zen teacher in Southern California. He told me that I should meet the monk Nyogen Senzaki and gave me his address at the Miyako Hotel in the Japanese section of Los Angeles.

I went immediately to see Senzaki Sensei and was struck by his wonderful personality. I determined to study with him and returned to Northern California for my wife. We both began to do zazen under his guidance.

Senzaki Sensei never called himself a roshi. He had made efforts to bring a true roshi from Japan to meet with his students. However, these efforts had not succeeded, so he kept the Dharma alive as best he could by himself.

We sat in chairs and had very little instruction, except what we could gain from his teisho. Mostly we learned from his wonderful manner, his kindness, and his modesty. He gave us Buddhist names—mine was "Chōtan," meaning "Deep Pool."

Senzaki Sensei was widely read in Western literature and he especially appreciated Meister Eckhart, the thirteenth and fourteenth century German mystic. He quoted Eckhart to me:

> The eye with which I see God is the very
> same eye with which God sees me.

"Show me that eye!" said Senzaki Sensei. I worked on this koan very hard and one day I went to see him with an answer. Seated before him, I simply closed my eyes.

"Oh, ho!" he cried. "Well then, were does it go when you sleep?" I could not answer. I worked very hard on this second koan too, and years later, when I was doing Mu under other teachers, that old question would pop into my head.

I was studying for a master's degree in Japanese literature at the University of California at Los Angeles at this time, but my wife was unhappy in Southern California and we decided to discontinue our zazen with Senzaki Sensei and return to Hawaii where she could be near her family. Back in Honolulu, I took up the master's degree program in Japanese literature at the University of Hawaii, which I completed in 1950, writing my thesis on "Basho's Haiku and Zen." At this time our son, Thomas, was born.

I was anxious to return to Japan to do zazen, and I earned a fellowship for a year's study there with the help of Dr. D. T. Suzuki, who taught at the University of Hawaii during the summer of 1949. Once in Japan, I lived for five months at Zenkyō An in Kenchōji, Kitakamakura and attended classes as an auditor at Tokyo University. This was in the fall of 1950.

Dr. Shōkin Furuta and Dr. Blyth helped me to find residence at Zenkyō An and also to enter Engakuji for sesshin. This was my first experience at true zazen. I was already thirty-three years old, and quite stiff. The zazen hurt my knees so badly that I could only walk a few steps. Three weeks after this sesshin ended, I returned to Engakuji for *rōhatsu sesshin*, my knees still swollen from my November experience. It was true agony. I was in complete despair.

Asahina Sōgen Roshi and his monks were very kind, but foreigners were rare beasts at a Zen monastery in those days, and Zen teachers had little experience in dealing with them. I knew that Senzaki Sensei had a close relationship with the monk Soen Nakagawa at Ryutakuji in Mishima, so I wrote to Nakagawa *Oshō* and he invited me to visit his monastery.* With my interest in haiku, we immediately became friends and I attended the January sesshin at Ryutakuji, still in great pain, but was permitted to take *agura* and Nihonza positions, which enabled me to survive.

Asahina Roshi had tried to translate my "Eye of God" koan into Hui-neng's "Original Face and Eye," but the old master of Ryutakuji, Yamamoto Gempo Roshi, found this was too complicated for me, so he set me to work on Mu. In the dokusan room, I felt a little resistance to this change, but on returning to my cushions, I discovered what zazen really is. No longer was I aware that the cracks in the tile floor formed a weird pattern. I could sink at last beneath the surface of my mind.

I moved to Ryutakuji after the January sesshin and lived there until I returned to Hawaii the following August. It was a mixed experience. I took joy in studying with Nakagawa Osho—he encouraged me to write haiku and we had a memo-

*Nakagawa Soen (Roshi) is a poet who writes in both modern and classical styles.

rable trip to Kyoto, Nara, and Iga-Ueno in conjunction with his forthcoming installation as Roshi of Ryutakuji.

However, I was also unhappy at being separated from my wife and baby son Tom, and ultimately I became exhausted from the strain of keeping the schedule of the monastery. On a *takuhatsu* (begging trip) to Namazu City, I caught dysentery and I sat through the June, 1951, sesshin with this dreadful affliction, very ill indeed. As I look now at photographs of myself at this period, I can hardly recognize my features in what seems almost a death mask.

Nakagawa Osho, now Roshi, took me to a physician in Mishima who didn't help at all, so I sought aid from Dr. Blyth at his home in the compound of the Peers' School in Tokyo. He took me to his own physician who gave me antibiotics and cured the dysentery. However, I was still very weak and at Nakagawa Roshi's suggestion, I took time off and rested in a hotel on the Izu Peninsula. It wasn't all that restful. As the end of my year in Japan approached, I felt more and more oppressed with a sense of failure, despite the kindnesses of all my teachers and friends.

Just before my departure for the United States Nakagawa Roshi and I were walking on the Hongo near Tokyo University and happened to see a figure of Bodhidharma in the window of Morie Shōten, the well-known Buddhist bookstore. The Roshi insisted that I buy this figure and I was quite willing, as it was a most unusual and artistic piece. He embarrassed me by telling our friends this Bodhidharma would be the central figure in the temple I would establish in the United States. Such a thing was beyond my dreams. However, Bodhidharma accompanied me back to Honolulu, and later to Los Angeles, and then to Honolulu again.

Reunited with my wife and son, I found that my funds from the government, which were granted to me as compensation for my war experience, had expired, and to support my family

I went to work as a community organization executive in a town near Honolulu. My relationship with my wife had deteriorated during my absence in Japan and after two more years together, we agreed to separate. Fortunately, she and I have been able to become good friends in the passage of time, and I am blessed with a deeply rewarding relationship with our son Tom, now twenty-one and a senior in college.*

I left for the Mainland again in 1953 and resumed my study with Senzaki Sensei, but a combination of the strain of the past two years and the poor health I had brought back from Japan brought on a physical collapse. I was hospitalized for a time, then spent long months in convalescence.

Afterwards, I spent a year or so working for P. D. and Ione Perkins, the Asian booksellers where I had first learned of Senzaki Sensei, and then one of Sensei's students helped me to find a position at the Happy Valley School in Ojai, where I had searched in vain for Krishnamurti several years before.

During this period, I continued my zazen with Senzaki Sensei, but I found my relationships with people were quite frozen. I felt isolated and unable to communicate. Nakagawa Roshi visited the Los Angeles Sangha for a few months in 1954 and we had a fine reunion. But generally this was a sterile period.

I consulted with a psychologist for a year and then, upon moving to Ojai, with a psychiatrist. With the aid of the latter doctor in particular, I was able to loosen up a little, and to express my feelings. In February, 1957, Anne Hopkins, Assistant Director of the Happy Valley School, and I were married and we went to live in a beautiful adobe house with huge windows overlooking the walnut orchards of the Ojai Valley.

Anne and I took a trip to Hawaii and Japan that summer. In

*Thomas Aitken is today a school counselor employed by the Department of Education of the State of Hawaii.

Honolulu we found Tom, then seven years old, rather lonely for his father, and I too felt the desire to be closer to him, so we decided to move to Hawaii the following year.

Arriving in Japan, we spent two weeks at Ryutakuji, where we met the monk, Eidō Shimano (Tai San). He impressed us as an earnest and dignified young man who spoke good English, and it was evident that he was a favorite of Nakagawa Roshi. He expressed a strong desire to go to the United States and we agreed to help him.

I participated in a sesshin at Ryutakuji and Anne and I climbed Mt. Fuji with Nakagawa Roshi. The Roshi then took us to Tokorozawa where we sat for seven days in the historic August, 1957, sesshin with Yasutani Hakuun Roshi, where Akira Kubota and Tatsuō Hiyama had their kensho.*

This was Anne's first sesshin and she marks it as the first step in her Zen practice. For me, Yasutani Roshi was a revelation, for he seemed to be a distillation of pure energy. When the sesshin ended with the excitement of the two kenshos, I found myself in tears for having missed the experience myself, despite such a favorable opportunity.

We returned for our final year at the Happy Valley School, laying plans for our move to Hawaii. In May, 1958, Senzaki Sensei passed away at an advanced age and Nakagawa Roshi came to California and conducted two memorial sesshins with Sensei's followers. I served as *jisha* for the first of these sesshins, while the Roshi doubled as *jikijitsu*. I believe it was the first full seven-day sesshin conducted in a regular manner in the United States.

Emanuel Sherman, later to go to Japan as a Zen student, was jisha at the second sesshin, as Anne and I departed for our move to Honolulu before it began. Pauline Offner, who also

---

*Messrs. Hiyama and Kubota are today senior members of the Sanun Zendo in Kamakura, which is led by Yamada Koun Roshi.

went later to Japan as a Zen student, attended both of these early sesshins.*

During this visit of Nakagawa Roshi to Los Angeles, Anne and I consulted with him about helping Tai San come to the United States. The Roshi agreed to allow him to come the following year. We were delighted, partly because we would be able to keep our promise to Tai San and partly because we thought having him with us might encourage Nakagawa Roshi to come to the United States on a regular basis.

Anne and I arrived in Honolulu and looked around for something to do for a living. Finally we established a second-hand bookstore with specialties in Asian religion and Hawaiiana. I kept a record of all customers in Asian religion so that when Tai San could come we would have a list of people who might be interested in establishing a group.

However, Tai San became ill and his trip was postponed. I decided to try to start the *zazenkai* anyway and wrote to Nakagawa Roshi for permission. Pauline Offner, who by then was in Japan, came back through Honolulu on an emergency family visit and brought with her the Roshi's consent to our plans. Accordingly, we held our first meeting in October, 1959, in the living room of our home, with four people present, including ourselves. Bodhidharma was installed at last.

We met weekly until Nakagawa Roshi came to lead sesshin early the next year, 1960, and thereafter we met twice weekly, a schedule never broken and still maintained at the Honolulu zendo.

Nakagawa Roshi went on to California during his visit in the spring of 1960 and was instrumental in reviving Senzaki Sensei's old group, which had been dormant since his death. He conducted another sesshin on his return through Hawaii,

---

*These two Western Zen pioneers pursued separate careers as Zen students in Japan, and then went on separately to Southeast Asia where they became ordained as Buddhist religious. Both have since died.

and we felt our group was well established. In August of that year, Tai San was at last able to come and be leader of our zazen.

We were meeting at this time at our home near Koko Head, a crater whose Hawaiian name was partly the reason for the name Nakagawa Roshi gave to our zendo, "Koko An."* It was an inadequate place for meetings, however, and we sold out and acquired a larger place near the University of Hawaii, the present Koko An. It had a view of Diamond Head, another crater, a landmark of Waikiki Beach, and this partly influenced the choice of our organizational name, the "Diamond Sangha."†

Nakagawa Roshi returned in 1961 and held two sesshins with us again, the first at the old Koko An, and the second at the new place. At that first spring sesshin, I felt particularly determined. I sat up for a portion of several nights and found myself in rather a deep condition. I experienced a makyo in which I was seated on the floor of a huge old stone temple, with enormous pillars extending to a lofty ceiling. Very tall monks dressed in black walked slowly around me in a circle reciting sutras in deep voices. The total experience had the flavor of something from the ancient past.

On the afternoon of the fifth day, Nakagawa Roshi gave a great "*Katsu!*" in the zendo, and I found my voice uniting with his, "Aaaah!" In the next dokusan, he asked me what I now know was a checking question. I could not answer, and he simply terminated the interview. In a later dokusan, he said that I had experienced a little bit of light and that I should be very careful.

In his closing talk after sesshin, the Roshi said, "Someone got a little bit of light." I knew that he was referring to my experience, but I did not treat it very seriously. However, I

*"Koko An" means "The Small Temple Right Here" in Japanese.
†The name "Diamond Sangha" refers also to the *Diamond Sutra*.

found the ceiling of my mind to be infinitely spacious. Everything was bright and new. I felt that I had had a good sesshin.

Between the two sesshins in Hawaii in 1961, Nakagawa Roshi visited Los Angeles and New York, and at New York conducted his first sesshin on the East Coast, with the help of Dr. and Mrs. Paul Weisz and others of his followers. This laid the groundwork for future East Coast sesshins, and for some of the Zen organizations that flourish there today.

Following the second 1961 sesshin, we established the *Diamond Sangha* newsletter, now in its eleventh year. This publication has carried important articles on Zen over the years and was particularly useful in coordinating the early trips of the two Roshis, Soen Nakagawa and Hakuun Yasutani, and later in publishing papers on Zen practice by our advisor, Katsuki Sekida.*

Anne and I decided in the summer of 1961 that we would like more training in Japan, so we sold our bookshop, left the zendo in Tai San's care, and came first to Ryutakuji, and then, at Nakagawa Roshi's suggestion, to Taihei An in Sekimachi to work with Yasutani Roshi. Yasutani Roshi received us very kindly and he and his students quickly found us a nearby cottage and made us feel very much at home. We enjoyed our early morning visits to the zendo for dokusan and the periodic sesshin. We learned to appreciate life in the Japanese dimension, including daily visits to the public bath. We both gained much from our intensive practice and made treasured friendships with members at Sekimachi and at the Kamakura Zazenkai. Unfortunately, at this time I was quite sensitive to the tatami on which we slept, and I had frequent attacks of asthma, but I tried to ignore them and, as I recall, missed only a part of one sesshin.

*The newsletter came to an end and my talks and other pieces are now carried in our quarterly journal, *Blind Donkey*. The Diamond Sangha also publishes *Kahawai, Journal of Women in Zen*.

Toward the end of our stay, Philip Kapleau talked with me about Yasutani Roshi's willingness to go to the United States to lead sesshin. I discussed this with Yasutani Roshi. He confirmed this wish and expressed the desire to retire in Hawaii. We were delighted by this prospect and assured him we would do all we could to assist him.

Nakagawa Roshi was due to come to the United States again in 1962, but his mother passed away and he cancelled the trip, requesting that Yasutani Roshi go in his place. I believe he also entrusted Tai San's training to Yasutani Roshi at this time.

This began a long series of annual trips by Yasutani Roshi to the United States, ending only in 1969. When I think back on the sacrifice of time and energy that our old teacher made for us, I feel profoundly unworthy of all that dedicated and concentrated work on his part.

Before each sesshin, I would feel great anticipation, hoping that I could achieve the same level of spirit I reached in the first 1961 sesshin, but I never did. The Roshi was kind and encouraging, but in dokusan I would have nothing to say, and, secretly, I felt deeply discouraged. I seemed to be stuck in one place in my practice.

With the prospect of Yasutani Roshi retiring in Hawaii, we bought property at Pupukea on the rural side of Oahu and our members spent every weekend for a year repairing the little house and painting it for the comfort and pleasure of the Roshi and Satomi San.* We also cleared the grounds, started a garden, and planted fruit trees.

In 1964, Tai San accepted an invitation to move to New York, where he has since been successful in setting up the New York Zendo of the Zen Studies Society, and more recently has been instrumental in establishing a mountain center in up-

---

*Satomi Myōdō Ni, an elderly nun who was Yasutani Roshi's attendant.

state New York. Yasutani Roshi was faced with the prospect
of retiring in a foreign country without the services of a good
interpreter. Meanwhile, he was urged by his students in Japan
to postpone his retirement, so he decided to withdraw from
the Pupukea plan. We understood this situation and sold the
property.

Yasutani Roshi continued to come for annual sesshin in
conjunction with his visits to Los Angeles and New York. We
maintained our zazenkai without a resource member from Japan until June, 1965, when Mr. Katsuki Sekida, a lay student
from Ryutakuji, came to Koko An at Nakagawa Roshi's suggestion. Mr. Sekida has been with us ever since, though he is at
this writing temporarily in London with the Ryutakuji
branch there.*

From 1962 until 1969, I worked for the University of
Hawaii in administrative positions, mostly with the East-
West Center. This work took me to Asia on one occasion, but I
had only a few days in Japan. I did gain a broader perspective of
Buddhism, however, through visits to Buddhist countries in
South and Southeast Asia.

It must have been about 1966 or 1967 when I began to
notice that I could make sense of some koans. In particular, I
remember the case of "Yen-kuan and the Rhinoceros Fan."

> Yen-kuan: "Bring me the rhinoceros fan."
> Attendant: "It is broken."
> Yen-kuan: "In that case, bring me the rhinoceros." The at-
> tendant could not answer.†

It seemed to me an intelligent five-year-old child could
have brought that ugly old beast to Yen-kuan. At that time,

---

*Mr. Sekida retired to his home in Japan soon afterwards.

†This is part of Case ninety-one of *The Blue Cliff Record*. See Bibliogra-
phy.

however, I did not appreciate the attendant's initial response, "It is broken."

Mr. Sekida's talks and writings and personal counseling were especially helpful to me during this period. My zazen deepened as I came to value the samadhi aspect of Zen training.

In 1967, Anne and I discussed our own future retirement and investigated several possible properties on Oahu. One of our members moved to the island of Maui and on visiting her, we happened to find what seemed to be a very good parcel of two acres, with a little cottage, in a remote section of the island. We purchased this property and soon learned that the cottage had a history of being rented to young people who had dropped out of the main stream of conventional society. We continued this rental practice and on periodic visits came to know these young people, to appreciate their values, and to feel concern for their problems.

I am not sure just when we decided to establish a Zen center on our Maui property. The decision came gradually over the next year, I think, as it became more evident that the large number of disaffected young people who had migrated to Maui from Mainland United States might form a sufficiently large pool of potential members and, further, that their sincere interests might readily be turned to Zen.

In June, 1968, one of our Koko An members was graduated from the University of Hawaii and he offered to stay at the Maui house, to repair it, and to set up a zazen schedule. We agreed to this plan. For the next year, the atmosphere of the Maui house had a Zen flavor. It became known among the young people as the "Haiku Zendo." "Haiku," in this case, is the Hawaiian name for the district. I did not care for this name, partly because there already was a "Haiku Zendo" in Los Altos, California, so-called because it has places for seventeen people.* When we moved to Maui, we changed the name to "Maui Zendo," the name it still retains.

Finally, on July 1, 1969, I was able to retire from the University of Hawaii and move to Maui. Brian Baron, one of our old-timers at Koko An, moved over with me as work foreman, and two other Koko An people came with us on a temporary basis. Anne and Mr. Sekida joined us from Koko An in September. The program set up at that time has been slightly modified over two and one-half years to the following:

5:00 AM	Rise and wash
5:10	Zazen
5:50	Study period
6:30	Breakfast
7:00	Work meeting, cleanup, work period
9:30	Refreshment break
10:50	Work period ends
11:10	Zazen
11:50	Zazen ends
Noon	Dinner, short rest
1:00 PM	Work period
3:00	Work period ends, refreshment, rest
4:30	Zazen
5:10	Zazen ends
5:20	Supper, silent rest
7:10	Zazen (talks twice a week)
9:00	Lights out †

Meantime, back at Koko An, we rented the house to three people who agreed to keep it open for twice-weekly meetings. After a year, the Koko An members became independently strong enough so that some of them could take over as tenants

---

*The classical Japanese haiku poem contains seventeen syllables.

†The Maui Zendo has its own building and grounds now, a mile away from the old place, where Anne and I continue to live. The schedule has changed in a number of ways.

and the original renters moved out. So Koko An, too, is a residential Zen center, with members keeping a daily zazen schedule, while going out during the day to work or to college.*

My health, never very robust, became quite poor after the move to Maui. I found it very difficult to establish a regular monastic schedule with people who knew little of such matters and who were used to a more hedonistic way of life. My own lack of strength in matters of leadership was painfully evident to me. Also, I probably worked too hard in assisting with essential repairs and enlargements to the cottage. In any case, I was quite ill, off and on, for a period of about eighteen months. Nevertheless, with the help of Anne, Mr. Sekida, and Mr. Baron, the Maui Zendo kept its Dharma light burning steadily.

Mr. Sekida was very encouraging to me. It was his opinion that I had had kensho and he expressed this opinion to Yasutani Roshi at the Roshi's last visit to Hawaii, October, 1969, during our first Maui Zendo sesshin. The Roshi agreed to try me on koan work, but I had little confidence, and did only two miscellaneous koans during that sesshin. I was unclear about how to handle dokusan in this new dimension, and especially about what was meant by "showing" my opinion.

Nakagawa Roshi came for a brief sesshin in October, 1970, but this was an especially difficult time and I do not recall that I had any serious dokusan with him. He was scheduled to come twice for sesshin in October, 1971, but his own illness delayed the trip and he was not able to come to Hawaii at all. However, I attended a sesshin he conducted with Tai San in California in August, 1971. At that sesshin, Nakagawa Roshi took me through several checking questions and confirmed

---

*The program at the Koko An Zendo has never wavered. It now has a larger membership than the Maui Zendo. I visit there monthly for zazenkai or sesshin.

the opinion of Sekida Sensei and Yasutani Roshi regarding my kensho. We also went through a couple of koans from the *Wu Men Kuan* and I began to understand the dokusan procedure beyond Mu.

After sesshin, Nakagawa Roshi and I agreed that I should invite Yamada Koun Roshi, Dharma successor of Yasutani Roshi, to come to Hawaii on a regular basis. Anne and I had known Yamada Roshi in connection with our participation in the Kamakura Zazenkai ten years before, so we were highly pleased at this new plan.

Now, at this writing, we have completed two sesshins with Yamada Roshi in October, 1971, one at Koko An, and one at Maui. A member of the Maui group attained kensho and others in both groups made excellent progress. I feel a solid confirmation of my own kensho and am pursuing my study of koans as diligently as I can.

We find Yamada Roshi to be our true teacher, personally interested in each student, calling each by name, encouraging confidence in each, yet strictly requiring clear evidence of attainment. His teishos are a revelation to all. We can scarcely believe our good fortune that he has accepted us as his students and that he may be able to visit us for sesshin henceforth on a regular basis.*

As I look back over this willy-nilly Zen path, I realize that teachers, friends, and family have demanded from me the strength and direction which I thought I lacked in pursuing it. First there was Blyth Sensei and Senzaki Sensei, then Nakagawa Roshi, Yasutani Roshi, and Sekida Sensei, and now at last, Yamada Roshi, who has inspired me with a totally new life.

The Koko An members, and more recently the Maui Zen-

---

*Now aged seventy-five, Yamada Roshi continues to visit the Diamond Sangha periodically to check with our senior students and give teishos.

do members, with whom Anne and I live as elder sister and brother, have demanded a quality of leadership that we have at last begun to establish. The response of our ten resident members here on Maui has become warm and responsible over the months and years and today the Maui Zendo almost runs itself, with everyone taking his turn at the many household, garden, and zendo tasks. We are a true Zen family, taking deep pleasure in one another, and in our vital work of realizing essential nature together.

Throughout these twelve years since the Diamond Sangha was established in 1959, Anne has been a constant source of support and comfort to me. Nothing would have been possible without her encouragement. She bore the brunt of responsibility during my illnesses and never indicated even in the most difficult periods that all this effort might not be worthwhile.

I believe that my own ill health is behind me for a while. Perhaps it was partly a sort of Zen sickness, the festering of some potential that was not being fulfilled. With Yamada Roshi's trust in my capacity to progress in Zen, I feel confidence and happiness I never supposed I could attain. I am profoundly grateful to him, and seek only to justify his trust.

Maui Zendo, Thanksgiving Day, 1971

Afterword

Now almost eleven years have passed, and I reread this memoir with mixed feelings. I would not write it in this way now (I certainly would not use that word "kensho" so much), but it had relevance then and I am persuaded that it may be useful to new students now.

Looking back, I understand my "dark night" from 1961 to 1971 much better than I did a decade ago. My experience with Nakagawa Roshi in the first 1961 sesshin was not deep enough to give me significant insight and it took several more years of zazen to prepare me to really begin Zen practice. This kind of chronology is not usual but I do occasionally meet others with similar histories.

In the years following the end of this record I moved fairly rapidly through koan study. Yamada Roshi led sesshins in Hawaii frequently, and I visited him at the Sanun Zendo in Kamakura with Anne for lengthy periods during the years 1972–1975. The Roshi gave generously of his time, and I saw him at least once a day for dokusan, and of course more frequently during sesshin. Anne too made fine progress in her practice during this period.

In December, 1974, Yamada Roshi found me ready to teach independently. This has been my sole occupation ever since at the Maui Zendo and the Koko An Zendo, with periodic trips to the Sydney Zendo, the Ring of Bone Zendo, and to Tacoma, Washington, for occasional sesshins with Catholic friends. As I wrote eleven years ago, I feel profoundly grateful to Yamada Roshi, and my motive is simply to justify his trust.

A Table of
Chinese-Japanese Equivalents

NAMES AND BOOK TITLES

Chinese (Wade-Giles)	Chinese (Pinyin)	Japanese
Chao-chou Ts'ung-shen	Zhaozhou Congshen	Jōshū Jūshin
Chêng Tao Ko	*Zhengdaoge*	*Shōdōka*
Chü-chih	Juzhi	Gutei
Hua-yen	Huayan	Kegon
Kuan	Guan	Kan
K'uo	Kuo	Kaku
Ma-tsu Tao-i	Mazu Daoyi	Baso Dōitsu
Nan-ch'üan P'u-yüan	Nanquan Puyuan	Nansen Fugan
Pai-chang Huai-hai	Baizhang Huaihai	Hyakujō Ekai
Po Chü-i	Bo Jui	(Hakurakuten)
Shui-hsiang	Shuixiang	Zuizō
Tao Te Ching	*Daodejing*	*Dōtokukyō*
Ta Hsiung	Daxiong	Daiyū
Tao	Dao	Tō, Dō (Michi)
Te-shan Hsüan-chien	Deshan Xuanjian	Tokusan Senkan
Ts'ai Ken T'an	*Caigentan*	*Saikontan*
Wu-mên Hui-k'ai	Wumen Huikai	Mumon Ekai
Wu Mên Kuan	*Wumenguan*	*Mumonkan*
Yüeh-shan Wei-yen	Yueshan Weiyan	Yakusan Igen
Yün-mên Wên-yen	Yunmen Wenyan	Unmon Bun'en

Notes

1. Philip Kapleau, ed., *The Three Pillars of Zen: Teaching, Practice, Enlightenment* (Boston: Beacon Press, 1967), pp. 26–62.

2. Evening Message, Daily Zen Sutras, Diamond Sangha, Honolulu and Haiku, Hawaii.

3. See Yaichiro Isobe, trans., *Musings of a Chinese Vegetarian* (Tokyo: Yuhodo, 1926), p. 26. This work is out of print. See also Norman Waddell, trans., "A Selection from the Ts'ai Ken T'an." *The Eastern Buddhist,* New Series 2, no. 2 (1969): pp. 88–98.

4. See Kapleau, *The Three Pillars of Zen,* p. 28.

5. Kōun Yamada and Robert Aitken, trans., "Hekigan-roku," Diamond Sangha, Honolulu and Haiku, Hawaii. See Thomas and J. C. Cleary, trans., *The Blue Cliff Record,* 3 vols. (Boulder: Shambhala, 1977), 2: 345.

6. Kōun Yamada and Robert Aitken, trans., "Mumonkan," Diamond Sangha, Honolulu and Haiku, Hawaii. See Kōun Yamada, trans., *Gateless Gate* (Los Angeles: Center Publications, 1979), p. 13.

7. Robert Aitken, *A Zen Wave: Basho's Haiku and Zen* (New York: Weatherhill, 1978), p. 58.

8. See Hee-Jin Kim, *Dōgen Kigen: Mystical Realist* (Tucson: University of Arizona Press, 1975), pp. 78–80.

9. Haruka Nagai, *Makō-Hō: Five Minutes Physical Fitness* (New York: Japan Publications, 1972). This work is out of print.

10.   Yamada, *Gateless Gate,* pp. 25, 39.

11.   See Francis Dojun Cook, *Hua-Yen Buddhism: The Jewel Net of Indra* (University Park: University of Pennsylvania Press, 1977).

12.   See Hakuyū Taizan Maezumi, trans., *The Way of Everyday Life: Zen Master Dogen's Genjokoan with Commentary* (Los Angeles: Center Publications, 1978).

13.   Yamada and Aitken, "Mumonkan." See Yamada, *Gateless Gate,* p. 86.

14.   [Nyogen Senzaki], *Buddha and His Disciples: A Guide to Buddhism* (Tokyo: Sanyusha, 1932), p. vii. This work is out of print.

15.   Yamada and Aitken, "Mumonkan." See Yamada, *Gateless Gate,* p. 80.

16.   See A. F. Price, trans., *The Diamond Sutra,* Book One of *The Diamond Sutra and the Sutra of Hui Neng* (Boulder: Shambhala, 1969), p. 74; also D. T. Suzuki, trans., "The Kongyokyo or Diamond Sutra," *Manual of Zen Buddhism* (New York: Grove Press, 1960), p. 50.

17.   Prajñā Pāramitā Heart Sūtra, Daily Zen Sutras. See also Suzuki, "English Translation of the Shingyo," *Manual of Zen Buddhism,* p. 26.

18.   [Flora Courtois], *An American Woman's Experience of Enlightenment* (Los Angeles: Center Publications, 1971), pp. 22–23. This work is out of print.

19.   Eugene T. Gendlin, *Focusing* (New York: Everest House, 1978).

20.   Mealtime Veneration, Daily Zen Sutras.

21.   Occasionally, to emphasize the importance of step-by-step practice, a Zen teacher will speak of the "seed of Buddhahood," but this obscures the complementarity implicit in the Buddha's words: "All beings are the Tathāgata and their job is to realize what has always been true." Attaining Buddhahood is a silly idea. Water cannot be made more wet. See Zenkei Shibayama, *A Flower Does Not Talk* (Rutland, Vt.: Tuttle, 1970), pp. 89–90.

22.   Hakuin Zenji's "Song of Zazen." Daily Zen Sutras. See Suzuki, "Hakuin's 'Song of Meditation,'" *Manual of Zen Buddhism,* p. 152.

23.   See Yamada, *Gateless Gate,* p. 8.

24.   Yamada and Aitken, "Hekiganroku." See Cleary, *The Blue Cliff Record,* 1: 172.

25.   Great Vows for All, Daily Zen Sutras. See Suzuki, "The Four Great Vows," *Manual of Zen Buddhism,* p. 14.

26.   Hakuin Zenji's "Song of Zazen," Daily Zen Sutras.

27.   Shibayama, *A Flower Does Not Talk,* pp. 85–86.

28.   Yamada, *Gateless Gate,* p. 100.

29.   See Arthur Waley, trans., *The Way and Its Power* (London: George Allen & Unwin, 1949), p. 141. Check my translation against the Chinese text in Paul Carus, *The Canon of Reason and Virtue* (Chicago: Open Court, 1945), p. 27.

30.   Eido Shimano and Robert Aitken, trans., Shōdōka, Daily Zen Sutras. See Suzuki, trans., "Yoka Daishi's 'Song of Enlightenment,'" *Manual of Zen Buddhism,* p. 101; also, Nyogen Senzaki and Ruth Strout McCandless, trans., "Shō-dō-ka by Yoka-daishi," *Buddhism and Zen* (New York: Philosophical Library, 1953), p. 69. This latter work is out of print.

31.   Purification, Daily Zen Sutras. See Suzuki, "Confession," *Manual of Zen Buddhism,* p. 13.

32.   Prajñā Pāramitā Heart Sūtra, Daily Zen Sutras; see Suzuki, *Manual of Zen Buddhism,* p. 26.

33.   Mou-lam Wong, trans., *The Sutra of Hui Neng,* Book Two of *The Diamond Sutra and the Sutra of Hui Neng,* p. 51. Cf. Philip B. Yampolsky, *The Platform Sutra of the Sixth Patriarch* (New York: Columbia, 1967), p. 143 and note.

34.   Ti Sarana, Daily Zen Sutras. See Richard A. Gard, *Buddhism* (New York: Braziller, 1962), pp. 52–57.

35.   Yasutani Hakuun, "Inner Zen Teachings on the Three Treasures of Buddhism," Kenneth L. Kraft, trans. Unpublished ms.

36.   Enmei Jikku Kannon Gyō, Daily Zen Sutras. See Suzuki,

"The Yemmei Kwannon Ten-Clause Sutra," *Manual of Zen Buddhism,* p. 16.

37.   Hakuyū Maezumi, "Jukai: Receiving the Precepts," *The Ten Directions,* 2, no. 2 (1981).

38.   D. T. Suzuki, *Essays in Zen Buddhism, Third Series* (London: Weiser, 1976), Plate 33.

39.   Yampolsky, *The Platform Sutra of the Sixth Patriarch,* p. 148.

40.   See Nyogen Senzaki and Ruth Strout McCandless, *The Iron Flute* (Rutland, Vt.: Tuttle, 1961), p. 58. This work is out of print.

41.   Yamada and Aitken, Mumonkan. See Yamada, *Gateless Gate,* pp. 13–14.

42.   See Zenkei Shibayama, *Zen Comments on the Mumonkan* (New York: Mentor, 1975), pp. 20–21.

43.   "Mu" is the modern Japanese and Cantonese pronunciation. Standard modern Chinese uses the pronunciation "Wu."

44.   Shibayama, *A Flower Does Not Talk,* pp. 118–119.

45.   Kapleau, *The Three Pillars of Zen,* pp. 58–60.

46.   See Kapleau, *The Three Pillars of Zen,* pp. 54–57. See also Charles Luk, trans., *The Śūraṅgama Sūtra* (London: Rider, 1966), pp. 97–100. This work is out of print.

47.   Maezumi, *The Way of Everyday Life.*

48.   Kōun Yamada and Robert Aitken, trans., "Shōyōroku," Diamond Sangha, Honolulu and Haiku, Hawaii. Case 14. See also Thomas Cleary, *The Book of Serenity* (Weatherhill, forthcoming).

49.   Hakuin Zenji's "Song of Zazen," Daily Zen Sutras. See Suzuki, *Manual of Zen Buddhism,* p. 152.

Glossary

agura—(Japanese) tailor style of sitting, with both feet under the thighs

aikidō—(Japanese) the way of harmonizing the spirit; one of the Japanese martial arts

Amida—(Japanese) Amitābha

Amitābha—(Sanskrit) Buddha of Infinite Light and Life: central to Pure Land schools

anuttara samyak sambodhi—(Sanskrit) perfect, all-penetrating enlightenment

Arhat—(Pali) worthy; worshipful; one who is free from craving; ideal of Southern Buddhism

bodhi—(Sanskrit) enlightenment

bodhisattva—(Sanskrit) enlightened being; ideal of Northern Buddhism; one who forgets the self in working with others

bodhi tree—*see bodhi;* bo or pipal tree (*ficus religiosa*): the tree beneath which the Buddha meditated

Buddha—(Sanskrit) enlightened one; Śākyamuni; one of several figures in the Buddhist pantheon; a being

Butsu—(Japanese) Buddha

Ch'an—(*also Chan,* Chinese) Zen

ch'an-na—(*also channa,* Chinese) dhyāna

Dharma—(Sanskrit) law, religious, secular, or natural; the Law of Karma, phenomena; tao or way, teaching; pure emptiness

dhyāna—(Sanskrit) absorption; the form of meditation; *see samādhi*

dōjō—(Japanese) spot or place of enlightenment of the Buddha

139

under the bodhi tree; one's own place of enlightenment; the training center

dokusan—(Japanese) to go alone; to work alone; sanzen, the personal interview between rōshi and student

gacchāmi—(Pali) going to, will undertake

gasshō—(Japanese) to join the palms (in reverence or respect)

gāthā—(Sanskrit) verse of praise or succinct restatement of major points of the Buddha Dharma

guru—(Sanskrit) venerable; a preceptor

hakama—(Japanese) the skirt worn over a man's kimono

Hīnayāna—(Sanskrit) Lesser Vehicle, a Northern Buddhist term for the Southern Buddhism of Sri Lanka, Burma, and Southeast Asia

hōben—(Japanese) upāya

Hotoke—(Japanese) Buddha

jikijitsu—(Japanese) head of training and timer of zazen periods in the Rinzai *zendō*

jisha—(Japanese) head of logistical arrangements in the Rinzai *zendō*

Jōdō Shinshū—(Japanese) True Sect of the Pure Land; one of the Pure Land Schools, traced from Shinran Shōnin, 1174–1268

Kanzeon—(Japanese) Avalokiteśvara, Kuan-yin (Guanyin), Kannon; one who perceives sounds of the world; the incarnation of compassion; a bodhisattva of Northern Buddhism

karate—(Japanese) empty hand; one of the Japanese martial arts

karma—(Sanskrit) action; cause and effect; the world of cause and effect

"Katsu!"—(Japanese) the shout given by Zen teachers

keisaku—(Japanese) kyōsaku

kendō—(Japanese) the way of the swordsman; Japanese fencing

kenshō—(Japanese) to see nature; to see into essential nature; gnostic experience in Zen practice

ki—(Japanese) return, come down to, amount to, has source in

ki—(Japanese) breath; spirit; spiritual strength

kie—(Japanese) saraṇaṁ gacchāmi

kinhin—(Japanese) sūtra walk; the formal group walk between periods of zazen

kōan—(Japanese) relative/absolute; an expression of harmony of empty oneness with the world of particulars; a theme of zazen to be made clear.

kū—(Japanese) sky, śūnyatā, emptiness, the void

kyōsaku—(Japanese) keisaku, cautionary device; the flat, narrow stick carried by the monitor during zazen

Mahāyāna—(Sanskrit) Great Vehicle; the Northern Buddhism of China, Korea, and Japan (Tibetan Buddhism is often included in this classification)

mantra—(Sanskrit) a spell; expression of veneration

makyō—(Japanese) mysterious vision; a deep dream occurring in, or associated with zazen

Mu—(Japanese) no; does not have; Case One of the *Wu Mên Kuan,* often the first kōan of the Zen student

mudrā—(Sanskrit) seal; hand position

Makkōhō—(Japanese) The Method of Directly Facing; a system of stretching exercises

Mañjuśrī—(Sanskrit) Beautiful Virtue; the incarnation of wisdom; a bodhisattva of Northern Buddhism

Namu Amida Butsu—(Japanese) Veneration to Amitābha Buddha; the Nembutsu; mantra of Pure Land schools

Myōkōnin—(Japanese) The Subtly Pure People; a gnostic movement in the Pure Land tradition

Nichiren—(Japanese) the Nichiren Sect, traced from Nichiren Shonin, 1222–1282

Nichihonzan Myōhōji—(Japanese) sub-sect of Nichiren, traced from Fujii Nichidatsu, 1885–

Nihonza—(Japanese) Japanese sitting; seiza

nirvana (nirvāna)—(Sanskrit) extinction; extinction of craving; in Northern Buddhism: the wisdom presented in the world of phenomena

Ōbaku—(Japanese) the Ōbaku Sect, a reintroduction of Rinzai Zen into Japan after it had mixed with Amitābha pietism

oshō—(Japanese) father, the priest's title

pāramitā—(Sanskrit) perfection, Buddhahood

prajñā-pāramitā—(Sanskrit) perfection of wisdom

Rinzai—(Japanese) the Rinzai sect, traced from Lin-chi I-hsüan (Linji Yixuan), c. 866.

rōhatsu (ō) sesshin—(Japanese) the sesshin of eight days in great cold; the sesshin that commemorates Shakyamuni Buddha's enlightenment, December 8

rōshi—(Japanese) venerable teacher

samādhi—(Sanskrit) concentration; the quality of meditation; *see dhyāna*

Sanbō Kyōdan—(Japanese) Order of the Three Treasures; the Zen sect traced from Yasutani Hakuun, 1885–1973

Sangha (Saṃgha)—(Sanskrit) aggregate; Buddhist priesthood; Buddhist fellowship; fellowship; harmony of Buddha and Dharma

saraṇa—(Pali) shelter, home, refuge; freedom from conditioning

saraṇaṁ gacchāmi—(Pali) undertake to find abode in; find freedom from conditioning with

Sarvodaya Shramadana—(Sinhalese) Awakening of All through Sharing of Personal Energy; a community development movement in Sri Lanka based on Buddhism

seiza—(Japanese) quiet sitting; Japanese sitting; an alternative posture for zazen

Seiza Shiki—(Japanese) The System of Seiza; physical and mental culture through the practice of seiza

Semmon Dōjō—(Japanese) Special Training Place; a Rinzai Zen temple where monks or nuns are trained

sensei—(Japanese) teacher

sesshin—(Japanese) to touch, receive, or convey the mind; the Zen retreat, usually seven days

Shariputra (Śāriputra)—(Sanskrit) the disciple to whom the Heart Sutra is addressed

shōken—(Japanese) first view; the first interview between rōshi and student

skandas—(Sanskrit) compounding elements of being; things perceived and levels of perception

Sōtō—(Japanese) the Sōtō Sect; traced from Tung-shan Liang-chieh (Dongshan Liangjie), 840–901

sūtra—(Sanskrit) classical works; sermons attributed to the Buddha; Buddhist scriptures

takuhatsu—(Japanese) to show the bowl, the walk taken by monks or nuns through towns near the temple to accept gifts of money or rice tatami—(Japanese) the heavy 3 × 6 foot mats used as flooring in traditional Japanese homes and temples

Tathāgata—(Sanskrit) thus come (or go); one who thus comes; a Buddha

teishō—(Japanese) to present the shout; the rōshi's Dharma talk

Theravāda—(Pali) The Way of the Elders; modern Buddhism in South and Southeast Asia

Ti Saraṇa Gamana—(Pali) Taking the Three Refuges; the ceremony of making one's home in Buddha, Dharma, and Sangha

upāya—(Sanskrit) appropriate or skillful means; compassionate and wise action

Yajñadatta—(Sanskrit) Enyadatta, a mythological lunatic

zafu—(Japanese) sitting cushion; the cushion for zazen

zazen—(Japanese) seated meditation; dhyāna; Zen meditation

zazenkai—(Japanese) zazen meeting; a lay Zen group

Zen—(Japanese) dhyāna; the Zen Sect; the harmony of empty oneness and the world of particulars

zendō—(Japanese) meditation hall

A SHORT LIST

Zen Buddhist Titles
In Paper Covers

First Books

Buksbazen, John Daishin. *To Forget the Self.* Los Angeles: Center
 Publications, 1977. The teachings of Maezumi Hakuyū Rōshi
 for beginners.

Gard, Richard A. *Buddhism.* New York: Braziller, 1962. Not for
 reading and not a paperback. Valuable for reference.

Kapleau, Philip, ed. *The Three Pillars of Zen.* Boston: Beacon
 Press, 1980. Introduction to the Zen of Yasutani Hakuun
 Rōshi.

Reps, Paul, ed. *Zen Flesh, Zen Bones.* New York: Doubleday,
 1957. Includes "101 Zen Stories" by Nyogen Senzaki.

[Sasaki, Shigetsu]. *Cat's Yawn.* New York: First Zen Institute,
 1947. Bound issues of the first American Zen journal.

Sato, Giei, and Nishimura, Eshin. *Unsui: A Diary of Monastic Life.*
 Honolulu: University of Hawaii Press, 1973. Endearing
 illustrations.

Suzuki, Shunryū. *Zen Mind, Beginner's Mind.* New York: Weatherhill, 1970. Talks for beginners and old-timers.

Watts, Alan. *The Spirit of Zen.* New York: Grove Press, 1958.
 D. T. Suzuki for the masses.

Commentaries, Essays,
and Translations by Contemporary Teachers

Aitken, Robert. *A Zen Wave: Bashō's Haiku and Zen.* New York:
 Weatherhill, 1979.

Hasegawa, Seikan. *The Cave of Poison Grass*. Arlington, Va.: Great Ocean Publishing Co., 1975. A commentary on the *Heart Sū-tra,* insightful but poorly edited.

Leggett, Trevor. *A First Zen Reader*. Rutland, Vt.: Tuttle, 1960. An early anthology of essays and talks.

————*The Tiger's Cave*. Boston: Routledge & Kegan, 1977. A commentary on the *Heart Sūtra,* etc., by Obora Rōshi, an otherwise unidentified Sōtō teacher.

Maesumi, Hakuyū, and Glassman, Tetsugen, ed. *On Zen Practice*. Los Angeles: Center Publications, 1976. Essays, translations, and commentaries.

————*The Foundations of Practice*. Los Angeles: Center Publications, 1976.

————*The Hazy Moon of Enlightenment*. Los Angeles: Center Publications, 1978.

Mitchell, Stephen, ed. *Dropping Ashes on the Buddha*. New York: Grove Press, 1976. Talks and letters of the Korean teacher, Seung Sahn.

Ross, Nancy Wilson. *The World of Zen*. New York: Random House, 1960. Another early anthology.

Sensaki, Nyogen, et al. *Namu Diabosa: A Transmission of Zen to America*. New York: Theatre Arts, 1976. Essays, letters, poems, and talks by Senzaki, Eido Shimano, and Sōen Nakagawa.

Shibayama, Zenkei. *A Flower Does Not Talk*. Rutland, Vt.: Tuttle, 1970. A commentary on Hakuin Zenji's "Song of Zazen" and other pieces.

Shimano, Eido, ed. *Like a Dream, Like a Fantasy: The Zen Writings of Nyogen Senzaki*. New York: Japan Publications, 1978.

Dōgen Zenji

Cleary, Thomas. *Records of Things Heard from the Eye of the True Teaching: A Translation of the Shōbōgenzō Zuimonki*. Boulder: Great Eastern, 1980. An anthology of Dōgen's short talks and sayings.

Cook, Francis. *How to Raise an Ox*. Los Angeles: Center Publica-

tions, 1978. Ten practice-oriented chapters of the *Shōbōgenzō,*
by Dōgen Zenji.

Kim, Hee-Jin. *Dōgen Kigen: Mystical Realist.* Tucson: University
of Arizona Press, 1975. Cogent scholarship.

Maezumi, Hakuyū. *The Way of Everyday Life.* Los Angeles: Center
Publications, 1978. Dogen Zenji's *Genjō-kōan* with
commentary.

Yokoi, Yuho, and Brian Victoria. *Zen Master Dogen: An Introduction with Selected Writings.* New York: Weatherhill, 1976. Generally does not duplicate Cook's work.

Kōan Study and Kōan Collections, Including Commentaries

Cleary, Thomas, and Cleary, J. C. *The Blue Cliff Record,* 3 vols.
Boulder: Shambhala, 1977. The Pi Yen Lu (*Biyanlu; Hekigan-
roku*) with Sung period comments.

Cleary, Thomas. *The Book of Serenity,* 3 vols. To be published by
Weatherhill. A translation of the Ts'ung Jung Lu (*Congronglu;
Shōyōroku*).

Hoffman, Yoel. *Every End Exposed: The 100 Perfect Kōans of Master
Kido.* Brookline, Mass.: Autumn Press, 1977. With comments by Hakuin Zenji. Professor Hoffman's own comments
are of doubtful value.

Miura, Isshu, and Sasaki, Ruth. *The Zen Kōan.* New York: Harcourt Brace, 1966. This is *Zen Dust,* as published by Harcourt
Brace, without the extensive notes of that more expensive
book.

Sekida, Katsuki. *Two Zen Classics: Mumonkan and Hekiganroku.*
New York: Weatherhill, 1977. The *Wu Mên Kuan (Wumen-
guan)* and the *Pi Yen Lu (Biyanlu).* Useful as a reference for the
translations.

Shibayama, Zenkei. *Zen Comments on the Mumonkan.* New York:
Mentor, 1975. The first commentary written for Western students on the *Wu Mên Kuan.*

Yamada, Kōun. *Gateless Gate: A Definitive Translation of the Mumonkan.* Los Angeles: Center Publications, 1980. Teishō for
Westerners by a modern teacher on the *Wu Mên Kuan.*

Translations of Talks, Essays, Poems, Letters,
and Sayings of Chinese and Japanese Teachers

(See D. T. Suzuki, *Manual of Zen Buddhism,* below.)

Blofield, John. *The Zen Teaching of Hui Hai.* New York: Weiser, 1972. Talks by a T'ang period teacher.

————*The Zen Teaching of Huang Po: On the Transmission of Mind.* New York: Grove Press, 1959. Talks by a T'ang period teacher.

Cleary, Christopher. *Swampland Flowers: The Letters and Lectures of Ta Hui.* New York: Grove Press, 1977. Teachings of a Sung period teacher.

Cleary, Thomas. *The Original Face: An Anthology of Rinzai Zen.* New York: Grove Press, 1978. Talks by Japanese teachers.

————*The Sayings and Doings of Pai-chang.* Los Angeles: Center Publications, 1979.

————*Timeless Spring: A Soto Zen Anthology.* New York: Weatherhill, 1980.

Hoffman, Yoel. *Chinese Radical Zen: The Sayings of Jōshū.* Brookline, Mass.: Autumn Press, 1978. A useful reference, despite the rough translation and dubious comments.

Sasaki, Ruth, et al. *A Man of Zen: The Recorded Sayings of Layman P'ang.* New York: Weatherhill, 1976. Stories of the best-known Chinese lay Zen student.

Shigematsu, Soiku. *A Zen Forest: Sayings of the Masters.* New York: Weatherhill, 1981. An anthology of Zen quotations with the Chinese text.

Wong, Mou-lam. *The Sutra of Hui-nêng.* Boulder: Shambhala, 1969. Published with *The Diamond Sūtra* (below). Outdated but useful.

Yampolsky, Philip B. *The Platform Sutra of the Sixth Patriarch.* New York: Columbia, 1967. The accepted translation with Chinese text of Hui-nêng's teachings.

Sutras

(See D. T. Suzuki, *Manual Of Zen Buddhism,* below)

Chang, Garma C. C. *The Buddhist Teaching of Totality: The Philoso-*

phy of Hua Yen Buddhism. University Park, Penn.: 1971. A commentary on the *Hua Yen Sūtra;* Useful, but not as reliable as Cook's *Hua-yen Buddhism,* also available from Penn. State.

Price, A. F. *The Diamond Sutra.* Published with *The Sutra of Hui-nêng* (above). Boulder: Shambhala, 1969. Outdated, but useful.

D.T. Suzuki

Barrett, William, ed. *Selected Writings of D. T. Suzuki.* New York: Doubleday, 1956.

Suzuki, D. T. *Essays in Zen Buddhism,* First Series. New York: Grove Press, 1961.

————*Essays in Zen Buddhism.* Second Series. New York: Weiser, 1970.

————*Essays in Zen Buddhism.* Third Series. New York: Weiser, 1970.

————*Manual of Zen Buddhism.* New York: Grove Press, 1960. Outdated, but useful translations of the principal texts of Zen Buddhism, including the *Heart Sūtra* and the *Diamond Sūtra.*

————*Living by Zen.* New York: Weiser, 1972. Includes references to Christianity from a Zen viewpoint.

Design by David Bullen
Typeset in Mergenthaler Garamond #3
by Dwan Typography
Printed by Spilman Printing
on acid-free paper